Department of English Local History

OCCASIONAL PAPERS

Fourth Series   Edited by Charles Phythian-Adams and Harold Fox

Number 3

Church and Chapel in the North Midlands: *Religious Observance in the Nineteenth Century*

K.D.M. SNELL
Lecturer in Regional Popular Culture,
Department of English Local History,
University of Leicester

LEICESTER UNIVERSITY PRESS 1991

© K.D.M. Snell 1991

First published in Great Britain in 1991 by Leicester University Press
(a division of Pinter Publishers Ltd)

Editorial offices
Fielding Johnson Building, University of Leicester,
University Road, Leicester, LE1 7RH

Trade and other enquiries
25 Floral Street, London, WC2E 9DS

British Library Cataloguing in Publication Data
A CIP cataloguing record for this book is available
from the British Library
ISBN 0–7185–2038–6

Filmset by Mayhew Typesetting, Bristol, Great Britain
Printed and bound in Great Britain by Billing and Sons Ltd.

Contents

List of figures

List of tables

Chapter 1

Quantification and Religious Historiography

The historical study of religion has been reluctant to adopt quantitative methods and to use them to refine current orthodoxies. When one thinks of the advances made in demography, in some branches of economic history, in historical geography, or in quantitative social history, one is struck by the relative absence in religious and local cultural historiography of the novel techniques used to considerable effect in other historical sub-disciplines over the past twenty or so years. One author even went so far as to comment that 'The history of the empirical investigation into religion in this country over the last hundred years is littered with examples of dogmatic and general conclusions based on very shaky evidence.'[1] Methodological innovation in this subject seems to have slipped between the disciplinary isolation of a few interested geographers, and the scepticism of some religiously committed historians towards the evident secular bias of religious sociology and its methods. This is despite the fact that the historiography of nineteenth-century religion is replete with arguments and statements, usually expressed through the use of literary or impressionistic evidence, which are nevertheless of an essentially quantitative and statistically testable nature, and ought already to have been so tested, elaborated and extended on a larger scale. In many cases such arguments have even used a derivative quantitative terminology without the empirical evidence and analysis usually associated with it.

Where quantitative methods have been employed by religious historians, these have frequently been simply descriptive, with a summary outline intent. They have in particular been used to describe denominational growth patterns as based upon the trends in membership statistics for different denominations, or to outline the geographical strengths of different denominations using the published county tables of the 1851 Religious Census and some of the later local censuses. There are of course some other exceptions to the general picture of methodological shyness; and the detailed nature of the published data is such as to have allowed illuminating work to be based on it.[2] Furthermore, analysis of the occupational and class support for different denominations is slowly advancing, although the scope for detailed comparative work here remains very large.[3] Simple occupational and class generalizations remain very current in the historiography, continuing to inform and promote older arguments on the political dimensions of different denominations, or on whether 'Methodism' did or did not prevent 'revolutionary' behaviour. Current research on Nonconformist and Anglican baptismal and other registers will in due course hopefully enhance subtle understanding of the occupational religious cultures in different areas, and the involvement or non-involvement of various elements of the working class in different forms of dissenting religion.[4]

However, it remains the case that the subject is dominated by historiographical views which lack much systematic attempt at statistical verification. Nor has there been detailed regional comparison and explanation of any period using analytical quantitative methods. Yet it is clearly desirable to be able to specify exactly (in a language which lends itself to precise comparison) what relationships existed between the strength of different denominations, how marked these relationships were, how (and then why) they differed across regions, how they changed over time, and how they varied between specific denominations within the broad groupings of old and new dissent, or within Methodism itself. In due course, it would then become possible to examine the extent to which other factors may have influenced or been associated with such denominational relationships in particular areas, and of course with the tendency to secularization which so worried Horace Mann and his contemporaries: factors such as urbanization or the percentage of the population still rural-based, political behaviour as manifest in voting patterns, regional patterns of literacy, the nature of landownership, occupational and economic structure, the local age structure of the population in particular periods, and so on.

I wish here to reconsider some of the arguments usually encountered on denominational proximity or regional reciprocity, to adopt some different approaches to material in the 1851 Religious Census, and to extend analysis of the occupational basis of denominations. I shall focus attention upon the North Midland region as a test case. By the 'North Midland region' I mean the area so defined in the 1851 census, comprising the census registration districts of Leicestershire, Rutland, Lincolnshire, Nottinghamshire and Derbyshire. In using these county names I shall be employing the boundaries taken for the purpose of the 1851 census, which were dictated by registration-district boundaries, and which do not of course in all cases exactly coincide with the conventional county boundaries of that or a later time. It will be suggested that arguments current in religious historiography need to be qualified in a number of ways with regard to parts of the North Midlands thus defined, and probably elsewhere. I hope to suggest methods and results which can be developed and tested further by others, and which can also provide a framework of possibilities within which to turn once more to the literary evidence and ask more specific questions of it.

We should first remind ourselves of the main issues involved. 'Scarcely anything', wrote Horace Mann, 'is more curious or more puzzling, than the attempt to trace the causes why particular doctrines or religious parties, should find one soil favourable and another adverse to their propagation and success'.[5] Since he wrote this some of the most commonly encountered and important hypotheses in nineteenth-century religious historiography have been concerned with the social, economic and denominational context in which dissent thrived, its geography, and then in particular how the growth of Wesleyan Methodism and its various offshoots was related first to the strength or weakness of the Church of England, and second to the regional presence of old dissenting denominations. The prevailing arguments are well known. Most are essentially pitched in terms of the county as the region studied, others take a smaller area, such as the union or registration-district data of the census enumerators. A few studies have gone further and argued their case at parish level.[6] Sometimes it is not clear what regional unit of analysis is being employed. Occasionally the assumption appears to be that the general arguments made are applicable at all feasible geographical levels, whether county, registration district or parish, or indeed any other intermediate regional level.

Let me first review the arguments based on county-level data. Tillyard for example, in his article published as long ago as 1935, which has now reached the status of 'the Tillyard thesis', argued that the counties in which the Methodist churches became strong were noticeably distinct and separate from the regions of old dissent in the form of the Congregationalists, Baptists and Presbyterians.[7] His data for the early twentieth century were of the number of full-time ministers in each county, and the number of people to each minister. Using county rankings based on this evidence, he argued that:

> A comparison of the two lists shows how complementary to the other denominations the work of the Methodists has been. Not one of the first twelve counties of the first list appears among the first twelve in the second list. Much the same thing applies to the end of the list. Of the ten counties at the bottom of the first list not one appears in the ten counties at the bottom of the second list.[8]

This argument for regional complementarity between old and new dissent is frequently found, usually based on Tillyard's findings. We should briefly consider how convincing the evidence for it currently is. The argument can be tested readily by correlation, and if Tillyard's hypothesis is correct, one would expect his figures to yield a high negative correlation between the county figures he gives for old and new dissent. This would clearly be a more appropriate method than the generalization from extreme rankings which he used. If his figures are calculated accordingly, the correlation coefficient produced is only -0.140, a figure which is insignificant. For what it is worth, it suggests that only about 2 per cent of the county variation in the Methodist churches can be explained by the county strengths of the old dissenting sects for which he provided figures. One might make a similar calculation which would most favour his case: correlating only the top ten and the bottom ten counties in his ranking, and ignoring the others (although this would be a very exceptionable and probably untenable procedure). Yet the negative coefficient resulting (-0.365), while more convincing than that for all the counties together, is still not at all strong. Another and more credible method than the latter would be to calculate the Spearman's rank correlation coefficient for his figures, as based upon the ranked position of each county, using the same figures. This result is only -0.080, which is entirely insignificant and again shows an almost complete lack of a relationship between the two sets of figures on which he founded his argument. Far from demonstrating the validity of 'the Tillyard thesis', his own figures show an absence of a firm inverse association between old and new dissent. It is surprising that an argument based on them is taken seriously by many religious historians. There may well be an historical association of the sort he argued for, and there are plausible intuitive reasons to suppose that something of the sort existed. But clearly, it is not adequately demonstrated in his own figures, and the case remains to be proven.

I shall return to the use of correlation to consider the association between different denominations.[9] Views like Tillyard's are found in some other authors. The well-known argument to similar effect of Robert Currie is often cited, and was again largely based upon county data:

> whilst the older dissent generally grew strong where the Church of England was strong, deriving (at least historically) much of its membership directly from the Church of England, Methodism grew strong where the Church of England was weak, and recruited from those sections of the population that Anglicanism failed to reach. . .the bulk of Wesleyan membership and the greatest sustained Wesleyan growth occurred in precisely the areas where the Church of England was weakest.[10]

According to this view, it was the Church of England's position which was crucial, and which is held to explain most about the geographical incidence of old and new dissent. The argument that the location of Methodism should be interpreted against the prior backcloth of Anglican strengths and weaknesses is a staple of religious historiography. For some authors, Nonconformity generally (grouping old and new dissent together) is seen as occupying regions of only nominal Anglican presence. For others, prior Anglican strength is felt to have a crucial bearing mainly on Methodist expansion. Few authors have delved in statistical detail into the regional interrelations of more specific denominations; although presumably many would agree that it was the divisions within Methodism itself (rather than the relation of Methodism to the Anglican Church) that appear to have mattered most to many chapel communities at the time.

Generalizing with the more broadly drawn categories however, Gilbert has argued that nonconformity was generally successful

> only where the Church was either too weak or too negligent to defend its

traditional monopoly of English religious practice. There was an important inverse relationship, in short, between the decline of 'Church' religiosity and the proliferation of 'Chapel' communities in the period preceding the Anglican reforms of the 1830s.[11]

He stressed that 'The demographic and economic revolutions damaged the parochial system, and enlarged the context for Nonconformist growth, not by creating but by proliferating the kinds of situations in which the machinery of the religious Establishment broke down.'[12] Such situations were of course found most abundantly in urban areas, in the north, in upland regions like the Peak District, in the newly drained fenland areas, and in the industrial villages and towns which developed rapidly during and after the eighteenth century, such as the many mining, quarrying and framework-knitting villages of the North Midland region which concerns us.

This essentially twofold explanatory framework, common to much writing, is a feature also of the more detailed investigations by Alan Everitt, using such sources as *The Imperial Gazetteer*, undertaking to understand what local conditions facilitated the growth of 'dissent'.[13] While Everitt had much of value to say about the varieties of dissent, one is nevertheless presented with a relatively sophisticated version of basically the same 'either–or' dichotomy: the Anglican Church or Nonconformity: in some types of parish the former could maintain its hold; in other parishes certain conditions enabled chapels to be built and 'dissent' to thrive. This dichotomy in historiographical thinking (which groups all dissent together) is a common feature of current arguments, necessitated by some sources. It was of course found at the time, as suggested by the cruder literary case of Charles Kingsley's Squire Lavington, who 'confined his disgust to sly curses at the Methodists (under which name he used to include every species of religious earnestness, from Quakerism to that of Mr. Newman)'.[14] Certainly it has enabled some convincing and illuminating historical points to be made – in Everitt's case taking religious local history forward considerably at the parochial and *pays* levels of analysis. However, deployed alongside virtually any type of literary evidence, and with the prevailing simply descriptive quantitative techniques, it is doubtful whether the inevitable analytical bluntness of this method will be improved upon. One of its main limitations is to concentrate attention upon the relationship between Nonconformity and the Anglican Church; in so doing deflecting analysis away from the relations within Nonconformity itself, and giving to the Anglican Church a centrality in the explanations used which its strength in some areas would not warrant.

Even using an analytical framework of this nature, there have been dissenting or qualificatory arguments made to the views of Tillyard or Currie. Coleman for example, in one of the more detailed analyses to date of the 1851 Religious Census data, has suggested that there was 'no firm inverse relationship between levels of Anglican practice and levels of Nonconformity. In some areas, both did well; in other areas, both badly.'[15] Perhaps the two coincided to a greater extent than is

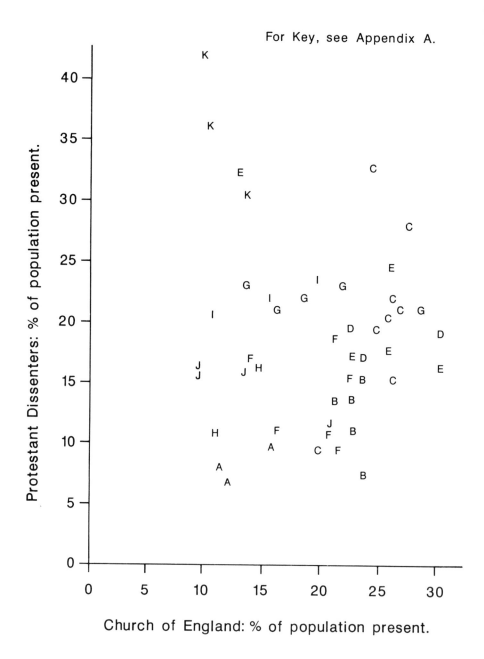

Figure 1 Percentage of the population present at the most numerously attended
service. Census Sunday, 1851: Church of England and Protestant
dissenters. England and Wales, by county.

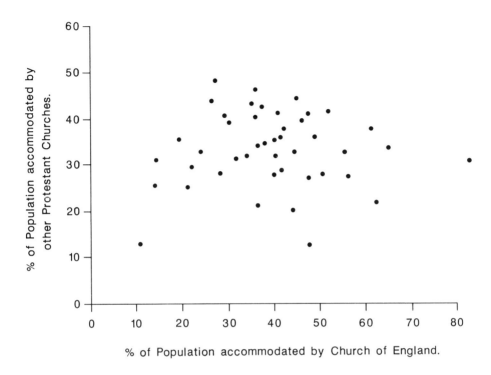

Figure 2   Percentage of registration-district population accommodated by the
Church of England, and by the other Protestant churches, 1851. North
Midlands.

appreciated. 'Where God builds a church the devil builds a chapel', the
proverb tells us – and maybe there were more potential meanings to this
open to the historian than has traditionally been apparent. However,
Gilbert demonstrated in a convincing manner the extent of Anglican
control in the south of England, and the difficulties the Church of
England had in establishing its authority in the areas of dispersed settlement of the north and west, in geographically and demographically large
parishes, in areas with significant non-agricultural occupational sectors, or
in regions of multi-nucleated settlement. Again, one notes how the
twofold possibility of the Anglican Church or dissent is a prevalent
feature in the argument.[16]

So let us examine this dichotomous conception of the problem more
systematically, staying for the moment within the terms still frequently
used. Fig. 1 shows the county strengths of the Church of England in 1851
(measured by the proportion of the population present at the best-
attended Anglican services on Census Sunday), plotted against the
county strengths of the combined Protestant dissenting denominations.
There is quite evidently no secure relationship at all between the two.
Protestant nonconformity taken as a whole, at this county level, had

clearly not generally become established where the Church of England was weakest. Nor is it possible to generalize that the strengths and weaknesses of the two coincided: that counties were arranged on a gradient suggesting that some were simply more 'religious' and others more secular than others, as a strong positive correlation would have implied. Certainly, different regions of the country had very varied strengths of the Church of England and of the other denominations, and this can be examined with reference to the key to the scattergrams in Appendix A. However, beyond that consideration, which will not detain me here, little can be said overall at this level of the relation between these two broad religious groupings.

Nor indeed does there seem to be any suggestion in the North Midland region itself that Protestant nonconformity was positively or negatively associated with the Church of England. Fig. 2 shows for the region the registration-district strengths of all the combined Protestant churches (measured by the percentage of the registration-district population they could accommodate) plotted against the strengths of the Church of England similarly measured. From the random results (r = 0.049) it is evident again that no argument could be made to the effect that 'dissent' generally flourished where the established church was weak. The same conclusion is reached if attendance figures for the North Midlands in 1851 are used: for example, if the major dissenting denominations' figures in Appendix C are totalled and correlated against the data for the Church of England the result again is random (r = −0.043). At the least, a consideration of these issues using the general concept of 'dissent' or 'Nonconformity' (combining all the multiplicity of Protestant dissenting denominations within it, as is common in the historiography) is a clumsy and unsharpened procedure which appears to suggest virtually no relationships between the respective strengths of the two entities being examined.

It is hardly surprising that disagreement occurs among historians on the associational, or geographical, relationships between such broadly drawn religious groupings, and that inexactitude of generalization is common. The use of county-level data itself cannot make for very precise analysis, and we have seen that Tillyard's argument is as yet very poorly evidenced. Accordingly, I want here to explore the matter much further, to look in more detail at the North Midland census region, to consider also the more southern counties of England, to investigate occupational and class differences as well as regional ones, and to see whether a more precise and convincing argument can be made on the corresponding strengths and weaknesses which existed in 1851 between the different religious groups in these counties. I hope that the methodological possibilities suggested, and some of the results, may provide scope for this angle of research to be refined and enlarged in due course.

Chapter 2

The 1851 Religious Census: Problems and Possibilities

The Religious Census of 1851 has been discussed frequently by historians, and its strengths and shortcomings have been sufficiently established so as not to warrant detailed assessment here. The conclusions of virtually all commentators on the adequacy of the census are perhaps best summarized in Inglis's words: 'For a study of the comparative support given to different denominations in the same area, and of variations in the support given to any particular denomination from place to place, the census offers a fairly adequate index.'[1] In fact, there may have been more discussion of the source *as a source*, than there have been systematic attempts to analyse it in any comprehensive manner.[2] The census referred to religious attendance and accommodation on Sunday, 30 March 1851. The enumerators provided detailed information from each parish on the places of worship of each denomination, on the number of sittings available, and the numbers attending morning, afternoon and evening services held by different denominations during that day. Average attendances over a recent period were also given, and used in final aggregations in the relatively few cases where actual Census Sunday attendance figures were absent. In the published census, information was provided at the registration-district or union level, and the figures were aggregated for each historical county, as conventionally defined.

Some data was provided of trends in chapel and church-building in the early nineteenth century; but the information available is for the most part an indication at a particular time of the accommodation and attendances for each denomination. In other words, it cannot be used to look at trends over time, except of course via comparison with other different sources, such as the Compton Census of 1676, the Evans list of 1715, visitation returns, the returns of the numbers of places of worship of 1829 (where they survive), or the less comprehensive religious censuses made later by the *British Weekly* in 1886, or by the *Daily News* in 1903.[3] The data is most suited to a consideration of the relative strength and geographical situation of each denomination at the time of the census. I shall use the registration-district data here, covering the total 44 registration districts in the North Midland counties, and will analyse also, but in less detail, the 173 districts of Surrey, Kent, Sussex, Hampshire, Berkshire, Wiltshire, Dorset, Devon, Somerset and Cornwall to consider the statistical association of the different denominations.

For this purpose, a number of measures can be derived from the published data. There is first the number of places of worship for each denomination, and the various calculations which could be based on that information: for example, calculations on the availability of places of worship provided by each denomination per thousand inhabitants. Second, the percentage of the population of each registration district which could be accommodated can be calculated for each sect, using the total sittings data provided. Third, it is possible to relate the total number of attendances at all services on that Sunday (or, for example, the maximum number of attendances at any one service) to the population of the registration district. Finally, one can calculate the total attendances for each denomination as a percentage of total attendances for all denominations, to give a 'percentage share' measure. Measures such as these give different indications of the 'strength' of each denomination, and, with the obvious exception of the fourth measure, lend themselves readily to correlation and to cross-verification to establish their reliability.[4] They have been calculated in various ways by other authors, notably by Inglis, Coleman and Gay. There are small problems in the use of the figures, which are susceptible to different resolutions or correction by different authors. The merits of the possible measures are open to debate, although it will be seen that the measures mentioned above can be checked against each other in such a way as to demonstrate their considerable reliability.

The main difficulty in establishing exact figures from the published data involves the corrections needed to cope with cases where data was absent, either for 'sittings' (i.e. accommodation available) or for attendances. Many attempts to use the data have ignored this problem, treating it as slight and largely inconsequential.[5] In most registration districts there were a few omissions from the published tabulations of either sittings or attendances, and in some cases, of both. The omission was notified by footnotes to the census tables. In the North Midland counties the number of sittings was not returned for 241 of the 3,627 places of worship (6.6 per cent); and the number of attendants was not returned for 194 of these places of worship (5.3 per cent).[6] It is clearly desirable to attempt correction of the published figures to take account of these omissions, however laborious this may be. The approach devised here for both sittings and attendances has been to correct the data by interpolating missing values based on the calculation of the mean values for that denomination in that particular registration district. Alternative forms of correction are possible, either of a much cruder nature or using methods based upon the denomination-specific ratios which can be calculated between sittings and attendance figures. It is likely that such a method in most cases provides slightly more accurate figures, but the method becomes impossible or irreparably convoluted in cases where neither sittings nor attendance data are available, and then one has to fall back upon the method of interpolating mean values.[7] A method inconsistently applied to prepare the figures may carry some dangers of bias which are best avoided. In view of the advantages of a consistent method applied throughout, the method reliant upon the interpolation of mean values has been used.

The two most revealing statistics to be derived as indications of the strength of each denomination are the percentage of the population which could be accommodated by each denomination (as based on the 'sittings' data), and the maximum or total attendances for each denomination expressed as a percentage of the total registration-district population (what some historians have termed the 'index of attendance'). The former calculation using sittings is unproblematical to make, but has the disadvantage of providing a misleading impression of the strength of some churches in some areas. This is notably so for the Church of England, for example in parts of East Leicestershire, where church capacity in partially depopulated pastoral areas was abnormally large in relation to the population in 1851. In some urban areas, a recent church-building programme could also result in problematical figures which are unrepresentative of denominational strength. Because of the historically recent growth of Nonconformity compared with the Anglican Church, and the consequently closer match between dissenting congregations and church size, a potentially serious bias could be built into any analysis which used only the statistics based upon the 'sittings' data.

The second possible calculation mentioned above, using the attendance figures, obviates this difficulty. It brings problems of its own, however. The most obvious is that there was an overlap between the attendants at different services for any one denomination, and even across denominations. It was common in some areas, for example, for a person to attend more than one service on Sunday, either of his or her own church or chapel, or to attend perhaps an Anglican service in the morning, and a dissenting service in the evening. The Rector of Swaby, for example, reported of

> one circumstance in particular, which will affect all calculations of this nature, and what is all but universal in this part of Lincolnshire at least, the attendance of members both at church and the (Wesleyan) chapels. . .few attend the church or chapel exclusively.[8]

It was noted that services were arranged accordingly, except in some cases where the Primitives deliberately arranged their own services to coincide with those of the Anglican Church, for example at Welton-le-Wold. There the Primitives'

> afternoon service clashed with that at church and in the evening when the Wesleyan Methodists met, the Primitives also had a service. The Primitive Methodists and some other nonconformist groups do not seem to have moved between church and chapel in the same way as the Wesleyans. Commitment to them may have involved a greater degree of separation from the main stream of community life, including attendance at the established church.[9]

Because of these difficulties involving overlapping attendants with divided loyalties, the denominational figures which can be calculated are of total *attendances*, rather than of total *attendants*, for there is no way in which the latter figure can be ascertained from the data available. Horace Mann, the author of the census report, suggested a calculation for each sect which summed the total morning attendants, half the afternoon attendants, and a third of the evening attendants, to give an overall figure for the number of separate attendants, and to compare different denominations.[10] This method has been used by some historians. However, for quite obvious reasons any such calculation is very inadequate, and if used in a regression analysis would introduce very serious biases. For example, the Anglican services were generally best attended in the morning, yet the new dissenting congregations were largest in the evening. Mann's fractions appear almost to have been devised to put the bravest face on the Anglican performance. (Over England and Wales, 48 per cent of Anglican attendances were in the morning, 16.3 per cent in the evening. The respective percentages for the Methodists were 29.7 and 44.3.) The method used here, of taking total attendances as a guide to the strength of each denomination, is clearly preferable to Mann's approach, and seems best suited to the derivation of figures which aim to measure the relative strength of each denomination. An alternative approach, also preferable to Mann's, would be to use the highest of the three attendance figures provided for each denomination. Again there are problems with this, lying in the different ratios for each sect between morning, afternoon and evening figures, which need not detain us here. In view of these problems, I have used total attendances over the whole day, but it should be stressed that we are dealing with attendances, rather than attendants. In so far as the analysis here deals only with the comparative or relative strength of each denomination, and does not involve making any statement about the total numbers of separate individuals attending the services of any particular sectarian grouping, the use of total attendances is largely unproblematical.[11]

As a way of checking the reliability of the census returns, it would be desirable to see whether measures such as the two mentioned above, based upon 'sittings' and 'attendances', are predictably consistent when assessed against each other. Because of the large size of some Anglican churches, in relation to their actual or even possible congregations – one thinks, for example, of the rural depopulation which had left some Midland churches stranded as lonely witnesses to previous pre-enclosure activities on the surrounding ridge and furrow – and because of the importance of the Church of England figures in many of the calculations one would wish to perform, one should initially concentrate on checking the Anglican figures. Of all the denominations, these are the most likely to be misleading as a guide to denominational strength, mainly because the potential 'sittings' space had frequently been predetermined such a long time before, when the churches had been built. Calculations based on 'sittings' data in 1851 would in some cases provide a poor reflection of demand, as in retrospect William Cobbett's writing had demonstrated.[12]

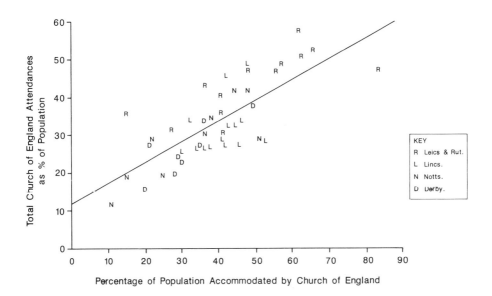

Figure 3 Total Church of England attendances as % of registration–district
population, and % of registration–district population which could be
accommodated by the Church of England. North Midlands.

Fig. 3 shows a scattergram of the Anglican 'sittings' (accommodation)
data, and its 'attendances' data, calculated as outlined above, for the 44
registration districts in the North Midland region. The registration
districts of each separate county have been distinguished in the scattergram to facilitate the recognition of each area, and to suggest at a
glance how the counties differed from each other. The approach is
instructive not only to assess the reliability of the figures, but also to test
one's a priori suppositions about the relationship between the availability
of religious accommodation and actual religious attendance. It is
immediately apparent that the fit between the two sets of figures is
reassuringly tight, and that the figures can accordingly be seen as
mutually strongly supportive. (The correlation coefficient is 0.781, significant at the 0.001 level.) It is also the case that the most urban unions lie
above the regression line, while the most rural ones fall below it. This is
what one would expect: that the 'attendance' data would be high relative
to accommodation data in the towns, and low in the rural areas.

The two unions which appear most obviously out of line are both in
Leicestershire: Leicester itself (14.5 per cent on the x axis), and the rural
union of Billesdon (83.4 per cent on the x axis). The latter was an East
Leicestershire union containing churches catering for a number of largely
depopulated parishes. Accordingly, one would expect the 'sittings' data
(showing the percentage of the population which could be accommodated) to be unreliably strong as an indicator of the strength of the

Table 1 Correlation coefficients for each denomination between the percentage of the population in each registration district which could be accommodated by that denomination, and the total attendances for that denomination expressed as a percentage of the registration-district population.

Church of England	0.781
Wesleyan Methodist	0.939
Primitive Methodists	0.958
Other Methodist sects	0.938
Baptists	0.960
Independents	0.936

Anglican Church. In Leicester, the figures are less easy to explain, and either the sittings data appears to be unreliably low, or the attendance data unreliably high. There may be faults in census enumeration or tabulation which explain this, or it may reflect a genuine feature of the town's religious practice.[13] However, despite some grounds for caution in the use of the data for these two unions, perhaps especially for Leicester, the overall picture is of the reliability of these measures to test the relative strength of the Anglican Church in the 44 unions.[14]

It is possible to show even more strongly the same general conclusion for the other denominations when treated like this. Table 1 shows the results of correlating the two sets of data in this way for the major denominations. It can be seen that the two sets of denominational figures are very strongly correlated for every denomination, the other denominations being much more highly correlated than even the Church of England. This feature was a product of their more recent growth, producing a closer match between the sittings and attendance figures. Interestingly, the old dissenting figures appear to be as reliable as those for the Methodists, perhaps suggesting the greater adjustability to changing circumstances of those older denominations compared with the Church of England. (These findings are also extremely close to correlation results between the raw census data of total attendances and total sittings, without reference to registration-district population.) The findings are highly reassuring for the use of the census in the way adopted here, and for the use of such figures for many other questions which historians may wish to investigate. Despite the largely untested objections a few authors have raised concerning the use of the census data, the results of this test suggest that we can have considerable confidence in the internal consistency of the religious data of the 1851 census.[15]

Chapter 3

The Geography of Religious Dispersal

Let me turn to the geographical spread of denominations, as based upon the index of attendance. This is mapped in Figs. 5 to 9. Fig. 4 gives the location of the North Midland registration districts. Concentrations of different religious denominations can easily be seen. The Wesleyan Methodists were particularly strong in north Lincolnshire; the Primitives were conspicuous there also, and in Derbyshire. Methodism generally was very weak in south Leicestershire and Rutland.[1] The Anglican Church was prominent in a large area of Leicestershire, and also strong

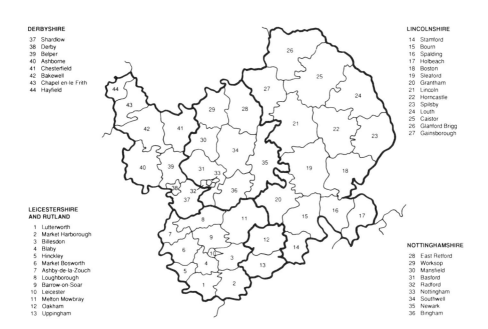

DERBYSHIRE

37 Shardlow
38 Derby
39 Belper
40 Ashborne
41 Chesterfield
42 Bakewell
43 Chapel en-le Frith
44 Hayfield

LINCOLNSHIRE

14 Stamford
15 Bourn
16 Spalding
17 Holbeach
18 Boston
19 Sleaford
20 Grantham
21 Lincoln
22 Horncastle
23 Spilsby
24 Louth
25 Caistor
26 Glanford Brigg
27 Gainsborough

LEICESTERSHIRE AND RUTLAND

1 Lutterworth
2 Market Harborough
3 Billesdon
4 Blaby
5 Hinckley
6 Market Bosworth
7 Ashby-de-la-Zouch
8 Loughborough
9 Barrow-on-Soar
10 Leicester
11 Melton Mowbray
12 Oakham
13 Uppingham

NOTTINGHAMSHIRE

28 East Retford
29 Worksop
30 Mansfield
31 Basford
32 Radford
33 Nottingham
34 Southwell
35 Newark
36 Bingham

Figure 4 North Midland registration districts.

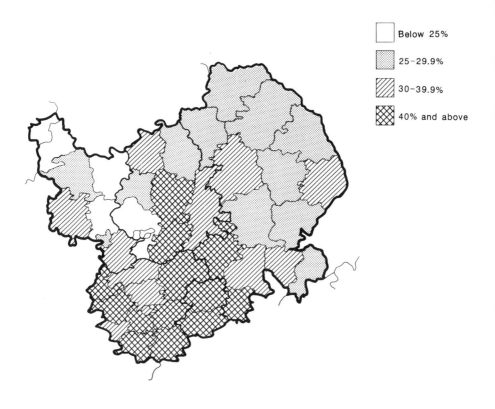

Below 25%

25-29.9%

30-39.9%

40% and above

Figure 5 Anglican total attendances as % of population.

in Rutland and southern and central Nottinghamshire.[2] The Independents were most salient in the south Leicestershire unions of Hinckley, Blaby, Market Harborough, Lutterworth, the larger towns, and a few Nottinghamshire and Derbyshire unions, while being largely absent from north-east Lincolnshire. The Baptists were strong in west Leicestershire and west Nottinghamshire, and even had a significant presence in the Anglican stronghold of Oakham. They were very weak across the whole of the northern areas of the three counties of Derbyshire, Nottinghamshire and Lincolnshire. The mapping of areas of strength in this way is helpful as a first step, but by itself provides only rather impressionistic conclusions on interdenominational proximities. What is clear however, is the way the very low presence of the Baptists and Independents in north and east Lincolnshire (this was also true for the Quakers and Unitarians) provided opportunities which seem to have been readily taken up by the two major Methodist sects. This was also the case in Bingham, and to a lesser extent of upland Derbyshire. Further, the exceptions to an account of Methodism 'infilling' into unions of Anglican

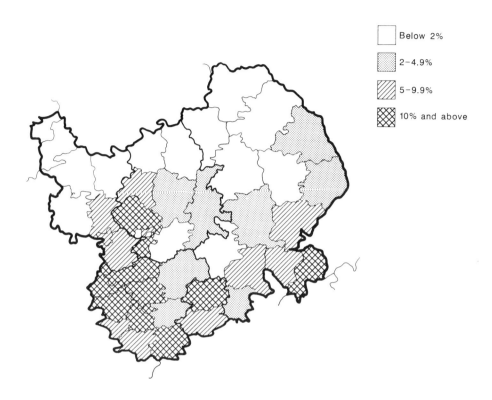

Figure 6 Baptist total attendances as % of population.

weakness are apparent: the registration districts of Melton Mowbray and Bingham being two of the most obvious examples.

It is also worth stressing the way in which the two main old dissenting denominations, the Independents and the Baptists, were by no means coterminous in their regions of greatest influence. The maps illustrate the way in which they were only very weakly regionally related over the entire area: Blaby and Market Harborough aside, there were substantial areas of mismatch between the two, especially in Derbyshire and west Leicestershire. If a more detailed analysis was made of all the separate older dissenting denominations which also used the 1676 Compton Census, it might be possible to show that the spread of the older dissenting denominations had a complementary logic of its own, similar to that which I shall document between old dissent generally and Methodism, and to a lesser extent within Methodism itself.

A further initial way of analysing denominational spread is to use denomination-specific 'coefficients of relative variation' for the calculated sittings and attendance data discussed above. Table 2 shows these measures, which convert the standard deviations of the figures for each denomination into measures of relative variation, by normalising the

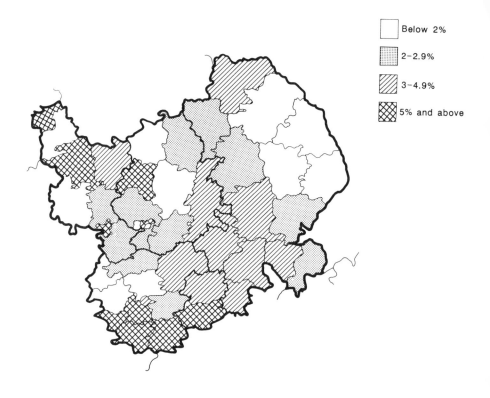

Below 2%

2–2.9%

3–4.9%

5% and above

Figure 7 Independent total attendances as % of population.

standard deviation on its own origin, namely the mean. These coefficients of relative variation, which are a denomination's standard deviation as a percentage of its mean, can then be compared across denominations. (Without being normalised in this way the standard deviations for each denominational mean cannot readily be compared; for they are measured in the same units as the mean, and in this instance will be liable to vary with the size of that mean.) The table suggests the comparative evenness of geographical spread for each denomination relative to its own strength.

Table 2 Coefficients of relative variation for the North Midland denominations

	Sittings data	*Attendances data*
Church of England	35.2	31.4
Baptists	82.9	88.2
Independents	84.1	107.2
Wesleyan Methodism	50.3	52.2
Primitive Methodism	75.2	76.0

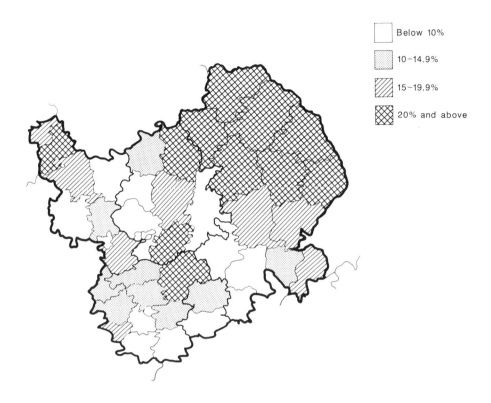

Below 10%

10-14.9%

15-19.9%

20% and above

Figure 8   Wesleyan Methodist total attendances as % of population.

There is a close match between results for the sittings and attendance data, again supporting the use of the religious census. While the variances or standard deviations of the Church of England figures were much greater than for any other denomination, the standard deviations of its figures relative to their larger averages were smaller (as shown in table 2). The Established Church was, in other words, more evenly spread relative to its average size than were the other denominations. And the Methodists (particularly the Wesleyans) varied less, relative to their size, than did the Baptists or Independents.

Many contemporaries such as Horace Mann raised the question of whether and to what extent greater provision of places of worship might raise religious consciousness and attendances. Partly with this in mind the Anglican Church, especially since 1835, had embarked upon a considerable programme of new church-building and repair under the auspices of the Ecclesiastical Revenues Commission. The aim was to make 'better provision for the cure of souls', particularly in urban and other neglected parishes; and it subdivided many parishes, providing them with new churches and clergy.[3] It can certainly be demonstrated that the availability of places of worship (that is, numbers of places of worship

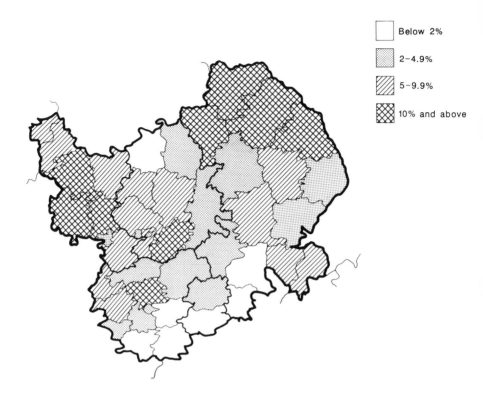

Below 2%

2–4.9%

5–9.9%

10% and above

Figure 9 Primitive Methodist total attendances as % of population.

calculated per thousand inhabitants of each registration district) was strongly associated with the index of attendance (that is, the total attendances for each denomination expressed as a proportion of the registration-district population). This is indeed what one might expect, although in historical terms it is unclear whether the availability of places had contributed to swell the attendances of the population, or whether historically strong Anglican or Nonconformist sentiment in different areas had itself led to a relatively high availability of places of worship. The correlation between the places of worship per thousand inhabitants and the denominational index of attendances was highest for the Primitive Methodists (0.915), and lowest for the Church of England (0.597). The other main denominations lay between these two, with the more recently established ones being highest – these after all had been the ones which had been best placed to plan with the more modern geography of population and religious demand in mind.

With regard to the issue of Anglican church reform, it is clearly significant that the Church of England shows the poorest match between provision of places of worship and apparent demand for them, and that denominations like the Primitives or Wesleyan Methodists (r = 0.858) performed best in this regard. Some of the Primitives' 'places' of worship were indeed best designated as 'places' (kitchens, granaries, barns, club rooms, shops, single rooms in private houses, and so on) rather than as 'chapels'. In this the sect had a flexibility and an adaptability to shifts in population movement and demand which the Anglican Church much more noticeably lacked; although this feature, shared with Methodism generally, was clearly associated with a propensity to schism. The flexibility of the circuit system of lay preaching was of course an additional and closely related feature favouring the advance of the Primitives, and conducing to the exceptionally tight match between its provision of places of worship and the demand for its particular form of dissent. Currie's account of the Primitives is instructive here:

> Like the Bible Christians, the Primitive Methodists were an alliance of different individuals and groups of evangelistic laymen. But although these groups were shortlived among the Bible Christians, they persisted in Primitive Methodism, where extensive geographical coverage enabled different leaders to form extensive local fiefs. These conditions encouraged the growth of what was called 'Districtism', i.e. *district* independence . . . district meetings had greater 'popularity and influence' than conference, which was 'little known by the rank and file and indeed wrapped in obscurity and mystery'. District meetings provided a basis for attacks on Conference, especially in the 1840s, and blocks of district delegates could greatly influence conference business. 'Districtism', like circuit independence, sought to counterbalance ministerial power in the denomination with lay power in the localities . . . the most important local unit was the circuit of chapels, governed by the circuit quarterly meeting . . . [which] had practical control of the running of the ministry.[4]

These 'rank and file' features of the sect go far to explain why the Primitive Methodists achieved such an immediate compatibility between local demand and provision, and the success consequent upon this. The contrast is especially noteworthy with the Wesleyan Methodists and the Church of England, whose hierarchical organizational structures were quite distinct and comparatively inflexible. Such denominational structures of authority and the related conflict over issues like camp meetings had been major reasons for the initial breakaway and formation of the Primitives.

It was also markedly the case that in registration districts where the Anglican Church had one or more churches or cathedrals of very large capacity, there its total number of churches was correspondingly low. Where its churches were on average small, they tended to be more numerous. In other words, there was a marked inverse relationship between the number of Anglican churches in each registration district, and their mean number of sittings ($r = -0.692$). This was true also for other denominations but to a much lesser extent. (For the Primitives, for example, with the smallest places of worship, the coefficient was -0.246. It was -0.286 for the Wesleyan Methodists.) In other words, the grandiose building ambitions of the Anglican Church in the past (while perhaps conferring upon it additional status) had in this other rather paradoxical sense been self-detrimental: for its unfilled, and often unfillable, larger edifices had seemingly contributed to a comparative sparsity of alternative Anglican accommodation in the neighbourhood which might often have been more readily accessible on foot. Inspection of attendances around some of the larger Anglican structures also suggests this. Other denominations, especially humbler forms of new dissent, more commonly escaped this negative influence which very grand ecclesiastical edifices had on the regional availability of places of worship, and so on the possibility of attendance. Of course, this was a problem the Anglican authorities were taking steps to remedy, with many comparatively small churches being built at and after this time. However, the Anglican Church would not have been aware in the terms used here of the exact nature of the historically evolved difficulty facing it, and the way its own situation in this respect differed from that of other denominations, and probably hindered it in comparison with them.

It is also clear in the North Midlands that compared with other denominations the Anglican Church was relatively backward in providing places of worship in the more urbanized areas, and most favourably placed with regard to religious demand in the most rural areas. This point has been made by others but should be further demonstrated and developed.[5] It is of considerable interest to look at the extent not only to which separate denominations flourished in 'urban' or 'rural' registration districts, or in town and country, but also to relate their strengths to measures which encompass the entire range from highly urbanized to very rural districts. The supposed association of Methodism with urban or market-town occupations – the supposedly lower middle-class support for Wesleyan Methodism – and the problems the established church had in gaining support in rapidly growing towns, are commonly found historiographical arguments. We can test these further for the North Midlands and throw more sharply focused light onto the differences between denominations in respect of their urban or rural incidence. Was it the case, for example, that Primitive Methodism was more rural-based than were the Wesleyan Methodists, and so likely to have had its most telling influence on the agricultural rather than the urban population? Was the Anglican Church more rural-based than the Primitives? – a question with interesting implications for agrarian labour historiography (so concerned with the influence of the Primitives). Furthermore, can it be firmly demonstrated that the more urbanized an area was, the more inclined its inhabitants were to secularized attitudes and religious non-attendance?

To answer such questions, measures of 'ruralization' and 'urbanization' were derived by using the ratio of each registration district's acreage divided by its 1851 total population, and vice versa. One such result therefore is that of 'acres per person' (which will be used to measure the extent to which a union was 'rural'), and the alternate ratio is that of 'persons per acre' – used here as an indication of the degree of urbanization of different unions. The two measures are of course inversely related

Table 3 The relation between 'urbanization' and
denominational strength

	Attendances	Sittings
Church of England	−0.235	−0.457
Independents	0.058	0.069
Baptists	0.183	0.144
Wesleyan Methodists	−0.332	−0.344
Primitive Methodists	−0.099	−0.180

(albeit not as strongly as one would expect), but it is nevertheless helpful to use both for analytical purposes. Table 3 shows the results of correlating the measure of 'urbanization' against the registration-district total attendances as a proportion of the population, and against the denominational sittings as a proportion of the population. The results are shown for each of the main denominations.

The results are consistent for both the 'attendance' and the 'sittings' data. It will be seen that of the five denominations the Independents and the Baptists were the most compatible with the urban environment, and that the Church of England and the Wesleyan Methodists were least so. Nor were the Primitives a movement to be associated in general with urban areas. Kendall was clearly right in commenting on

> that deeper denominational reluctance to fasten and concentrate its strength on the chief towns which marks the course taken by Primitive Methodism in the early years – a reluctance that was the outcome of habit and of preference, if not of deliberate policy.[6]

The urban origins and consolidation of the Baptists and Independents, and their very strong presence in Leicester and Nottingham, goes some way towards explaining the results for them. (The Quakers and Unitarians were also very strongly associated statistically with 'urbanization'. To a much lesser extent so were most of the other smaller breakaway Methodist sects.) In most cases the correlations using the 'sittings' data are more indicative than for the 'attendances' data. The implications of this are interesting. It appears that the Anglican Church, Wesleyan Methodists and the Primitives had staked out and built for a rural constituency to a greater extent than was warranted by urban potential and demand for them. Certainly these were the denominations (especially the Church of England and the Wesleyan Methodists) which were most obviously prone to be caught out by the rural exodus and the corresponding growth of the Midland cities.

The Baptists' and Independents' seventeenth-century urban origins and strengths, already suggested on the maps – and which could be strongly shown by mapping their places of worship – left them well situated to benefit from the changes in rural society which produced rural depopulation from about the mid-nineteenth century.[7] Around 1700 Celia Fiennes had commented on Leicester: 'Here are a great many descenters [sic] in this town.'[8] Later, and building on this earlier presence, there was to be a marked increase in Baptist churches in the town in the 50 years after about 1830. Leicester was widely and correctly known as 'the metropolis of dissent' in the nineteenth century, and its many excellent chapels still bear witness to this. Wesley had preached in Leicester 'to a multitude of awakened and unawakened'. He had to face only 'one feeble attempt to disturb' his preaching: 'a man was sent to cry FRESH SALMON at a little distance.' 'None took the least notice of him', he wrote, with embarrassed disdain.[9] He commented that Leicester was a place 'where I always feel much liberty, and yet see but little fruit', and the strength of old dissent in the town probably underlay such a statement: Wesley was evidently just a case of fresh salmon (or fruit) offered in place of the still edible old victuals.[10] The prior urban congruity of the Baptists and Independents in an important market and textile town like this must have been a major factor which allowed them to expand membership simultaneously with the growth of Methodism.[11]

The other side of this discussion can be pursued by considering how the strengths of the denominations related to what we may term 'ruralization' or the measure of 'acres per person'. We now expect the results to be the opposite of those shown in table 3. Table 4 demonstrates this very clearly.

Table 4   The relation between 'ruralization' and denominational strength

	Attendances	*Sittings*
Church of England	0.350	0.699
Independents	−0.178	−0.164
Baptists	−0.341	−0.216
Wesleyan Methodists	0.493	0.494
Primitive Methodists	0.111	0.225

It shows how strongly the Church of England's ability to accommodate the population, and to a lesser extent, its index of attendances, were associated with the rural areas. This association was also true of the Wesleyan Methodists. To a limited extent the Primitives too were associated with the more rural parts of the North Midlands, although when we examine the occupational structure of their followers we shall see that they had also a considerable presence in some of the growing industrial and mining districts. This probably explains why their association with the rural areas is shown here to be weaker than for the Wesleyan Methodists.[12] The Independents and Baptists were not primarily rural-based, and their relative position shown here helps to explain why their evangelistic efforts around this time seem to have been directed towards the countryside to a greater extent than was so for many other denominations.[13] The Quakers and Unitarians combined (using attendance data) were certainly inversely correlated with this measure of 'ruralization' ($r = -0.582$). This was also so for the other Methodist

Table 5 Correlation coefficients between the places of worship for each denomination (per 1000 inhabitants), and 'urbanization' and 'ruralization'

	Urbanization	Ruralization
Church of England	−0.419	0.754
Independents	−0.156	0.116
Baptists	−0.158	0.031
Wesleyan Methodists	−0.465	0.688
Primitive Methodists	−0.306	0.376

groups taken together; and in explaining their distinctiveness compared with the two major Methodist denominations it is surprising that more attention is not paid to their more urban affiliations.

A further question to raise in this context, and one which is helpful to elucidate the points made above, is to ask to what extent denominations differed in their provision of places of worship (per thousand inhabitants) in urban and rural contexts: in other words, to correlate the places of worship per thousand people for each denomination with the measures for 'urbanization' and 'ruralization'. We probably expect all denominations to be negatively associated with 'urbanization' in this test and to have more places of worship per thousand inhabitants in the more rural areas, but one is less able to predict how denominations vary between themselves in this. From the above discussion it might be anticipated that the provision of the Independents and Baptists would be least negatively associated with 'urbanization'. Table 5 shows this to be so for the North Midlands. What is of note is that the Wesleyans and the Church of England were almost equally strongly dissociated from 'urbanization' in their provision of places of worship. Thus, while the Church of England was doing badly in catering for the more urbanized populations, it could nevertheless have taken consolation in the observation (which never seems to be made) that the Wesleyan Methodists were doing as badly or slightly worse. Wesley may have taken his message to the dispossessed and forsaken 'heathen' of this industrializing society, as one often reads, but he appears to have done so more in the rural than the urban slums, despite his frequent dismissal of rural areas.[14] The more rural-based population was certainly better provided for than the urban by all three major denominations of the North Midlands: the Church of England, the Wesleyan Methodists and the Primitives.[15]

It is an axiom in the historiography of nineteenth-century religion that the towns were more secular, more irreligious, than the countryside. 'The most striking conclusion derived from the published statistics, both by the Victorians as well as modern historians, was the widespread religious indifference of the urban working classes', commented Soloway.[16] Some authors have placed great emphasis on this, in a few cases seeing it as one of the key features in a supposed process of secularization, which was quickened as the percentage of the national population in towns grew. The point can certainly be illustrated with evidence from some

larger towns and cities. However, by using the figures here for the inten-
sity of 'urbanization' and 'ruralization' in the North Midlands, it is possible to show that the effect of urban growth on the decline of religious
attendance can very easily be exaggerated. An index of overall total attendances as a proportion of registration-district populations was negatively
correlated with 'urbanization', as the literature might suggest, but only at
−0.157. The same index was positively correlated with 'ruralization', but
only at 0.147. These results are very low, and not markedly different.

In the registration districts of Leicester, Nottingham and Derby the
indexes for total attendances (all denominations) as a percentage of
population were 70.2 per cent, 62.8 per cent and 61.4 per cent respec-
tively. These percentages may be low by comparison with those for the
essentially rural and market-town unions of Market Harborough (90.3 per
cent), Blaby (88.2 per cent), Melton Mowbray (87.9 per cent), Market
Bosworth (84.3 per cent), or Gainsborough (77.8 per cent). But they are
higher than those for the mainly rural registration districts of Sleaford
(61.1 per cent), Bourne (54.9 per cent), or Chapel-en-le-Frith (52.7 per
cent). And other registration districts with large numbers of urban
industrial workers like Hinckley or Loughborough had indexes of total
attendances of 80.4 per cent and 77.0 per cent. Of course, there was a
great deal of industrial outwork in many Leicestershire, Nottinghamshire
and Derbyshire villages, and consideration is needed of occupational
regions and cultures to take account of this. On the basis of the figures
for this region it would clearly be inadequate to emphasize urbanization
as a factor diminishing overall religious attendance, or to draw too stark
a contrast between the general urban and rural religious sensibilities at
this time. As David Thompson commented on this period for Leicestershire:

> It is therefore a mistake to imagine that villages are necessarily places where
> church [i.e. all religious] attendance is strong. Some are; but others, particularly
> those with coalmining or domestic industry, have levels of attendance no better
> than towns the size of Leicester. . . . A rural migrant to a growing town . . .
> might well have come from a place where it was not normal to go to
> church. . . . Religious indifference does not begin with the move to the
> town.'[17]

There may even be grounds for saying that in some cases Nonconformist
faith commenced with the move to the town.

A more complex quantitative analysis of this matter than is currently
available, on a larger scale than the North Midlands, awaits further study.
This will need to distinguish between the separate types of town: where
they were situated, their sizes, their growth rates, and rates of migration
to them, the religious accommodation provided, their industrial occupational structures, their sex ratios, age structures, and rural hinterlands,
among other considerations.[18] It will also need to be wary of too great
an emphasis on the situation in London. Edward Denison's lament in the
1860s on 'the complete indifference of religion' in the East End was made
by many others.[19] But the most urbanized regions of the North

Midlands, at any rate, seem to have shared comparatively little of the irreligious habits which so struck contemporary observers of working-class areas in the Metropolis.[20]

Chapter 4

Statistical Relationships between Denominations

Let us now look in more detail at associations between the different denominations. If the Tillyard or Currie theses are correct for the North Midland counties, one will expect to find strong negative correlations between the Anglican Church and the Methodist denominations for each county, and a clear negative correlation overall for the counties combined. Tables 6 and 7 provide the correlation coefficients for the separate denominations against each other.[1] Table 6 uses the 'sittings' data, as outlined above; and table 7 is based on analysis of total attendances, that is, the 'index of attendance' – both measures are calculated by using the total population of each registration district. It is probably the case that table 7, based upon attendances, is more informative and reliable than table 6. Both tables are in clear agreement with each other on most important points. They suggest a number of conclusions regarding the religious experience of these counties.

It is immediately clear from the correlation of the Church of England against Wesleyan Methodism that any attempt to argue a simple inverse relationship between these two affiliations is simplistic, and probably obscures important regional variations. These variations exist to a marked extent even within the bounded area of the North Midlands. In Nottinghamshire, as shown in both tables, there was in 1851 a strong positive correlation between these two denominations. At the registration-district level the strengths and weakness of the one coincided with those of the other. What does this suggest? The finding is compatible (for this county) either with those historiographical views which stress the political conservatism and compatibility with establishment religion of the Wesleyans, or, alternatively, with a discussion of Wesleyanism which highlights the hostility it could receive on the ground from adherents to the Anglican church – a hostility which one might expect in situations where their strengths coincided, and where therefore they were probably felt to be mutually threatening. But it is not supportive of the common arguments that Wesleyan Methodism fitted into geographical vacuums created by the laxity or poor coverage of the Church of England, or of the

Table 6 Correlation coefficients between denominations, using the proportions of the population in each registration district which could be accommodated by each denomination, by county

	Leics. & Rut.	*Lincs.*	*Notts.*	*Derby.*	*Coefficient for all counties*
Church of England & Wesleyan Methodism	0.314	0.198	0.907	0.259	0.181
Church of England & Primitive Methodism	−0.260	−0.338	0.465	0.616	−0.149
Church of England & all Methodists (1)	0.118	−0.058	0.817	0.486	−0.010
Church of England & Baptists	−0.384	−0.474	−0.407	−0.149	0.077
Church of England & Independents	0.071	−0.087	−0.326	−0.586	0.078
Church of England & all old dissent (2)	−0.272	−0.532	−0.468	−0.599	0.037
Wesleyan Methodism & Primitive Methodism	0.287	0.500	0.581	0.367	0.546
Wesleyan Methodism & Baptists	−0.193	−0.344	−0.292	−0.188	−0.430
Wesleyan Methodism & Independents	−0.587	−0.610	−0.302	0.025	−0.449
Wesleyan Methodism & all old dissent	−0.639	−0.482	−0.396	−0.178	−0.572
All Methodists & all old dissent	−0.683	−0.438	−0.361	−0.263	−0.608
Primitive Methodism & Baptists	0.257	−0.226	−0.048	−0.784	−0.325
Primitive Methodism & Independents	−0.556	−0.319	−0.399	−0.049	−0.339
Baptists & Independents	−0.165	0.097	0.569	−0.267	0.183
1% significance level	0.684	0.661	0.798	0.834	0.384
10% significance level	0.476	0.458	0.582	0.621	0.251

Source: 1851 Religious Census, Registration-district 'Sittings' data for the North Midland region, adjusted for omissions in Enumerators' Returns.
Notes
1. Wesleyan Methodists, Primitive Methodists, Methodist New Connexion, Wesleyan Reformers, Wesleyan Association, Independent Methodists, Lady Huntingdon's Connexion. There were no Bible Christians established in these counties.
2. Baptists, Independents, Unitarians and Society of Friends.

way Wesley himself represented the role of his movement *vis-à-vis* the established church.

The Nottinghamshire picture is in obvious contrast to Lincolnshire, where in table 7 the inverse relationship predicted by Currie or Tillyard can be seen. Clearly for Lincolnshire the implications of the table would

Table 7 Correlation coefficients between denominations, using the total attendances for each denomination expressed as a percentage of the registration–district population, by county

	Leics. & Rut.	Lincs.	Notts.	Derby.	Coefficient for all counties
Church of England & Wesleyan Methodism	−0.068	−0.670	0.820	−0.406	−0.217
Church of England & Primitive Methodism	−0.585	−0.583	0.517	0.459	−0.349
Church of England & all Methodists	−0.391	−0.701	0.726	0.041	−0.406
Church of England & Baptists	−0.491	−0.207	−0.414	0.245	0.255
Church of England & Independents	0.374	0.300	−0.310	−0.607	0.325
Church of England & all old dissent	0.029	−0.088	−0.423	−0.176	0.348
Wesleyan Methodism & Primitive Methodism	0.290	0.572	0.421	−0.113	0.456
Wesleyan Methodism & Baptists	−0.366	−0.328	−0.348	−0.241	−0.454
Wesleyan Methodism & Independents	−0.507	−0.680	−0.286	0.077	−0.424
Wesleyan Methodism & all old dissent	−0.676	−0.511	−0.374	−0.189	−0.560
All Methodists & all old dissent	−0.636	−0.490	−0.136	−0.191	−0.581
Primitive Methodism & Baptists	0.392	−0.256	0.062	−0.309	−0.219
Primitive Methodism & Independents	−0.464	−0.428	−0.049	−0.175	−0.338
Baptists & Independents	−0.138	0.223	0.557	−0.050	0.248
1% significance level	0.684	0.661	0.798	0.834	0.384
10% significance level	0.476	0.458	0.582	0.621	0.251

Source: 1851 Religious Census, Registration-district total 'Attendances' data for the North Midland Region, adjusted for omissions in Enumerators' Returns.

be quite different than for Nottinghamshire. There is much firmer support in Lincolnshire for a hypothesis of Wesleyan growth having occurred in regions of poor Anglican strength; and surely in such circumstances the corollary would be a situation of more harmonious interdenominational politics in each district. That is, Wesleyan Methodism was less likely to have been perceived as a threat to the established church, and in areas where it became best established (like the unions of Horncastle, Caistor, Spilsby or Louth, where the Anglican index of total attendances was as low as between 26 and 34 per cent) Anglicanism was sufficiently weak for its reaction to be relatively muted. We shall return to such interpretative

aspects of the figures later, although it is as well to keep such implications in mind. The remaining county coefficients for the Wesleyans and
the Church of England are much weaker, and do not suggest a very
significant relationship between the two. The coefficients for the total
counties confirm this: the sign varies between the two tables, and in
neither case is the result strong. With the exception of Lincolnshire, the
view that Wesleyan Methodism grew in those regions where the Church
of England was weak is largely unsubstantiated; and the experience of
Nottinghamshire runs entirely contrary to such an argument.

Primitive Methodist growth was still under way in some areas at the
time of the census, and in considering its regional pattern and its association with other denominations, we need to bear this in mind. It is
probable that some further Primitive growth after 1851 was in regions
beyond those in which it had first expanded after the events of 1810–11,
and during its rural consolidation in the 1830s.[2] We also need to recall
the schismatic Methodist climate around the time of the census. The short
period since 1849 had been one of the most unfortunate in Methodist
history, with considerable anti-Conference sentiment, and with large
numbers of expulsions or 'resignations' taking place in 1849–50. Probably
over 100,000 members left the Wesleyan Methodists in this period.[3]
Many must have gone into the Primitive Methodists. In Lincolnshire
there was a short-term but significant rise in Primitive chapel-building in
1851.[4] However, we have seen already the very close match between the
Wesleyan Methodist 'sittings' and 'attendance' statistics (table 1); and this
gives one reason to believe that the impact of the schism of these years
on the reliability of the Methodist figures should not be exaggerated. The
tables indicate that Primitive Methodist regional variation at union level
was not markedly affected by the situational strength of the Anglican
Church, although there is certainly a clearer tendency for weaknesses in
the latter to be associated with its growth than was the case for Wesleyan
Methodism. The findings for Leicestershire and Lincolnshire in table 7
suggest this most noticeably. Nevertheless, the contrary pattern is
indicated for Derbyshire and again in Nottinghamshire. Over the entire
44 unions, there was only a weak or very weak inverse correlation
between the figures for the Primitives and the Anglican Church.

The other Methodist churches had a much smaller presence in these
counties, and indeed in many unions were entirely absent. Their incor-
poration with the Wesleyan and Primitives' figures, and a correlation
between a general 'Methodist' grouping and the Anglican Church does
not alter the picture presented here: of a weak and perhaps insignificant
negative regional association between Methodism and Anglicanism when
one considers all the unions combined in these counties. Nottinghamshire
is the notable exception, a county which runs entirely contrary to
historiographical expectations, and one where the pattern of new dissent
and its relation to the Anglican Church deserves further research at a
more parochial level.[5]

Some historians have argued the case for old dissenting congregations
having been strong in those areas where the Church of England was best

established. What do the calculations here suggest on this point? Of course, we need to bear in mind that the prior regional strength of groups like the Baptists or Independents may be poorly illustrated by data collected in 1851. In both these denominations, particularly for the 'Baptists', the enumerators included some groups which ought to be seen as part of the development of new dissent. It would in particular have been helpful to have had greater distinction in the census data within the 'Baptists'. Nevertheless, putting aside these points, there is only a slight correlation between the Anglican Church and the Baptists or the Independents when they are taken separately. Table 6 suggests overall (the 'coefficient for all counties') an almost total absence of correlation, although one might note the inverse correlation between the Baptists and Anglicanism in Lincolnshire. Table 7 however indicates that over all the unions there was probably a weak positive association between the Baptists or Independents and the Church of England. Because of the problems of the relatively outdated 'sittings' data for the Church of England, we may take the results of table 7 as more reliable, and as providing some limited support for this part of Currie's argument.

Results revealing very little statistical relationship between religious groups are as suggestive as those indicating strong correlations, particularly in the light of some of the more firmly advanced arguments in the historiography. There are however a number of marked correlations demonstrated within dissent itself. These are probably the most striking aspects of the two tables. In both tables there is an inverse association between Wesleyan or Primitive Methodism and the Baptists or Independents. This varies between the individual counties, but is especially marked between Wesleyan Methodism and the Independents in Leicestershire and Lincolnshire (both tables), between the Primitives and the Baptists in Derbyshire (table 6), and to a lesser extent between the Primitives and Independents in Leicestershire. There is overall a clear inverse relationship between Wesleyan Methodism and the Baptists (both tables), although it does not show up so strongly at the individual county level.

In some respects, these findings are to be expected. As the maps suggested, it seems evident that new dissent concentrated its efforts and gained strongholds in areas where the older dissenting congregations were relatively weak.[6] The point could be extensively documented with more anecdotal literary evidence. Most variations of the argument which views either old or new dissent as a viable option to the Church of England, to be embraced in that form which was readily available, gain support from these figures – a firmly established dissenting denomination frequently tended to exclude its rivals. There is little reliable correlation between the Baptists and the Independents, suggesting that their prior spread may have been largely independent and random with regard to each other. However, Nottinghamshire stands out as showing the highest correlation between these denominations, and overall in table 7 there is some evidence (particularly for this county) that they were both strong in the same unions by 1851. This was true for unions such as Nottingham,

Table 8 Partial correlation coefficients between selected denominations, holding the Church of England constant

	Leics.	Lincs.	Notts.	Derby.	Total
'Sittings' data (as calculated for table 6)					
Wesleyan Methodism & all old dissent	−0.606	−0.454	0.077	−0.030	−0.589
Wesleyan Methodism & Primitive Methodism	0.402	0.615	0.427	0.273	0.589
'Attendances' data (as calculated for table 7)					
Wesleyan Methodism & all old dissent	−0.676	−0.771	−0.052	−0.290	−0.529
Wesleyan Methodism & Primitive Methodism	0.309	0.301	−0.006	0.090	0.416

Mansfield, Lutterworth, Market Harborough, Hinckley, or Uppingham, and markedly so in Blaby. Because the data from 1851 regrettably joins together the various Baptist groups, and is later than one would wish, it ought to be handled tentatively when describing the historical patterns of old dissent.

I want now to turn briefly to the possibilities offered by a more sophisticated analytical technique. It is of interest to calculate the first order partial correlation coefficients between some of the major denominations, holding the influence of the Church of England constant. In statistical terminology, a partial correlation coefficient measures the amount by which a unit change in one variable can be expected to affect a second variable when the influence of a third (for example, the Anglican Church) is held constant.[7] The technique is useful to us because the correlation between, for example, the Wesleyan Methodists and the Primitives may be influenced by the Church of England's prior effect on each; and it would be instructive to remove such an influence of the Anglican Church to see whether the correlation is thereby affected in a significant way. Clearly, the variable one would wish to hold constant for our purposes here is the Anglican Church, for obvious historical reasons (it predates the others); and one would wish to do this in particular to examine the relationships between the Wesleyan Methodists and the Primitives, and the Wesleyans and the older dissenting denominations. Table 8 gives the partial coefficients that result from this exercise, and the results can be compared with the equivalent figures in the previous two tables. It can be seen that the total results for all 44 registration districts are not much affected when the figures are calculated in this way. For the most part the county-specific and overall partial correlation coefficients do not suggest that the Church of England's background and historical effect on denominations is distorting the simple coefficients between those denominations of tables 6 and 7, and the conclusions we might wish to draw from them.

It is also intriguing to ask how the Church of England may have

Table 9 Partial correlation coefficients between
Primitive Methodists and the Church of England,
holding the Wesleyan Methodists constant

		'Sittings' data		
Leics.	Lincs.	Notts.	Derby.	Total
−0.385	−0.515	−0.181	0.580	−0.301
		'Attendances' data		
−0.592	−0.328	0.331	0.455	−0.288

affected the registration-district location of the Primitive Methodists when one eliminates the influence upon both of the Wesleyan Methodists. It may be that the Primitives, as an increasingly more radical alternative to the Anglican Church than were the Wesleyan Methodists (and few would deny this, considering the beliefs of nineteenth-century agricultural unionism and the influences upon it), were proximately situated to the Church of England in the rural areas, and owed much of their influence and growth to a negative reaction against features of the established church which were felt to be repugnant by many of the essentially plebeian Primitive following: tithes, clerical magistrates, nepotistic and non-resident clergy, Tory clerical landownership, and so on.[8] Given the close connection between the origins of the Primitives and prior strength of the Wesleyan Methodists, it is of course advisable to hold the latter constant in any such calculations. Table 9 accordingly gives the partial correlation coefficients aimed at illustrating this relationship.

This sort of calculation is not without its interpretative difficulties, but it contributes an answer to the question asked which no amount of selective literary discussion and generalization would ever resolve. Over the whole 44 registration districts, putting aside statistically the influence of the Wesleyans, it is clear that the Primitives had tended to develop in those unions where the Church of England was relatively weak. One should not exaggerate this, but there is ground for interpreting the Primitives as a denomination with a propensity to fill vacuums left by the established church, rather than to rise successfully in local social, political and theological antagonism to that church. The regional positive correlation between Wesleyan and Primitive Methodism shown in table 8 does not obtain overall between the Primitives and the Church of England, although certainly this is not to deny that in some circumstances and areas such proximate association existed. This is exceptionally so in Derbyshire of the counties taken here, and the nature of Primitive and Anglican relations in that county may have been distinctive, presumably marked by the proximate origins of the sect. Probably the Anglican Church in other counties and regions, the Vale of Belvoir is a notable example, was for various reasons so hostile to the Primitives that by 1851 they had still failed to gain a significant foothold.[9] The strength of the established church in such areas (and its weakness in others, like parts

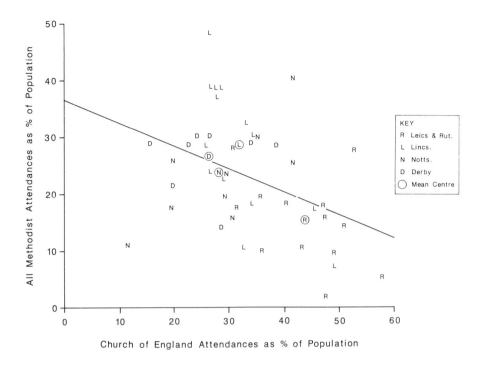

Figure 10   Church of England total attendances and total Methodist attendances, as % of registration-district population. North Midlands.

of Derbyshire), alongside the local social conditions favouring it, would be important explanations for the county partial coefficients observed. It is also evident and of considerable social and political interest (comparing tables 6 and 7 with tables 8 and 9) that the Primitives, while regionally associated with the Wesleyans, appear to have derived strength from the weakness of the Anglican Church to a greater extent than did the Wesleyans.

Clearly the relationship between different denominations expressed in the statistical ways used here were diverse, and it is frequently incorrect to argue in the hard and fast historiographical manner for particular patterns of association as generally applying. Different counties show variations and even opposite results from the overall picture provided by the 44 registration districts. The historiographical arguments currently deployed not only frequently lack an accuracy of qualified generalization, mainly because of their dependence upon literary sources, but also usually fail to notice the regionally different interrelationships shown here. It is evident from similar research in Northumberland, Staffordshire, Warwickshire and Shropshire, and in the counties further south to which we shall shortly turn, that such patterns within separate counties become even more diverse when one steps out from the North Midland region.[10]

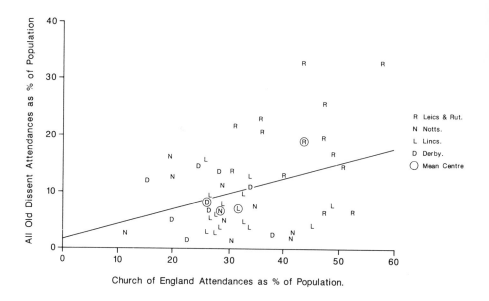

Figure 11   Church of England total attendances and total old dissent
            attendances, as % of registration-district population. North Midlands.

It is possible to demonstrate the distinctive regional patterns within the
North Midlands in a visually more appealing manner, by plotting each
union's co-ordinates on scattergrams. Only the data derived from the
attendance figures (as calculated for table 7) have been used for this. Fig.
10 shows the Church of England registration-district attendance data plotted against that for all the Methodist sects grouped together. The weak
overall negative correlation predicted in some of the historiography is
clear (r = −0.406). Also of interest is the regional patterning, and the
marked difference between the registration districts of Leicestershire and
Rutland (marked 'R') and the registration districts of the other counties.
The mean centres for Derbyshire, Nottinghamshire and Leicestershire are
very similar: that for Leicestershire and Rutland indicates the much
stronger position of the Church of England and the weaker Methodist
influence in this area.[11] In Lincolnshire the strength of the Methodists
exceed that in the other counties. Fig. 11 shows the same uniqueness of
Leicestershire, pointing in particular to the strength there of old dissent
(Baptists, Independents, Society of Friends, and Unitarians). Once more,
the mean centre for Leicestershire and Rutland is very differently located
than for the other three counties, setting their religious experience apart.
The other three counties were largely indistinguishable when one
considers the proximity of their mean centres. In fig. 11 some support can
be found for the view that old dissent, taken generally, was best
established in those ares where the Church of England was strongest (r
= 0.348); although one needs to note that this outcome is largely due to
the pattern of Leicestershire.

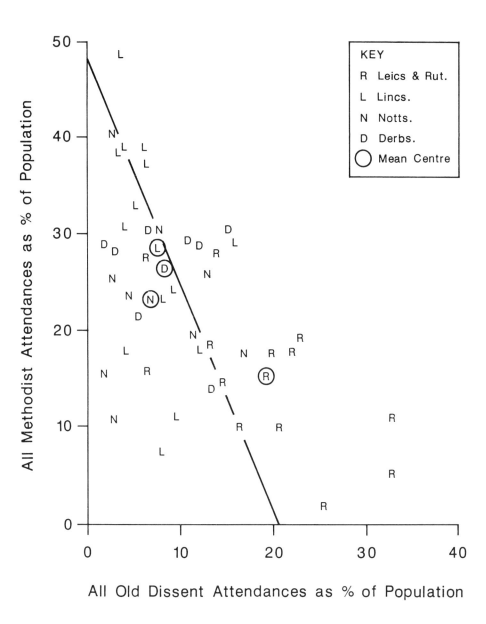

Figure 12   Total old dissent attendances and total Methodist attendances, as % of registration-district population. North Midlands.

When the North Midland counties' religious denominations are grouped in this simple threefold way – the Anglican Church, and old and new dissent – a number of general points become apparent. First, there is the strength of old dissent in Leicestershire (fig. 11 and 12), notably in the Market Harborough, Blaby and Lutterworth unions, where it seems to have all but excluded Methodist growth. Second, one is struck by the evidence of Methodist strength in Lincolnshire, particularly in the unions of Gainsborough, Glanford Brigg, Caistor, Louth and Horncastle (figs. 10 and 12). Such areas had a minimal presence of old dissenting denominations. With regard to the types of dissent, it is immediately evident from Fig. 12 that Leicestershire and Lincolnshire represented opposite extremes – one featuring old dissent, the other new dissent – with Derbyshire and Nottinghamshire filling an intermediate position. These extremes were such as to produce the negative correlation indicated in fig. 12 (r = −0.581). The scattergrams provide support at the general level for an argument that 'Methodism' was negatively correlated with old dissent, and to a lesser degree with the Church of England. It is clear too, if one takes all 44 unions together, that old dissent broadly shared its regional strengths and weaknesses with the established church. However, this general pattern was itself mainly due to the contrasting and distinctive religious emphases of Leicestershire and Lincolnshire. It should also be stressed that within the separate counties quite different statistical associations could obtain, especially in Nottinghamshire, and that the registration-district relationships at county level often suggest very little significant geographical correlation of any sort. It may be that this is heavily influenced by class or social differences between denominations, rather than those based essentially on region. Accordingly, it is to the question of the separate social structures of distinct denominations that I should now like to turn.

Chapter 5

Class, Occupation and Denomination: the Social Structure of Methodism

'We were the Church for the neglected and forgotten', wrote Kendall of his Primitive Methodist followers:

> All, whether friendly or otherwise . . . take for granted that our work lies amongst 'the ruder of the lower class' . . . that it is to labour on the great waste of poverty, ignorance, and crime, whose moral cultivation is to a great extent neglected by others. . . . Men said that our special mission was to the poor, the ignorant, the degraded . . . because they saw us doing it.

The views advanced by Kendall or Obelkevich that the Primitives represented a downward spread in the social scale of religious dissent, and a breakaway of the lay membership from the strictures of the Wesleyan authorities in areas which had already been much influenced by Wesleyan Methodism, seem very feasible in the light of the close regional identity of these two denominations.[1] To judge from the figures, the argument is one which may relate particularly to Lincolnshire, where we have seen that these denominations were closely associated. But Obelkevich's argument, made in relation to South Lindsey in that county, seems applicable elsewhere too, if perhaps to a lesser extent. The positive correlation between these two groups is strongly manifest in the overall figures and in the separate counties, except perhaps Derbyshire. It remains to be explained why Derbyshire (table 7) seems an exception here. The combined effects of its proximity to the north Staffordshire growth centres of the Primitives, the attraction to revivalists of its mining and upland occupational structures – such communities commonly showed a proclivity towards the Primitives or Bible Christians in other areas – and the somewhat weaker influence of Wesleyan Methodism in Derbyshire compared to Lincolnshire, may have been largely responsible for the difference.

The class difference rather than the regional contrast between the two major Methodist denominations should be further explored and demonstrated by looking at their social composition. For if it was the case, as suggested, that the Primitives had a differing social configuration

to the Wesleyan Connexion, albeit usually a similar geographical founda-
tion, this will have interesting implications not only for an understanding
of the relation of Methodism to other forms of dissent, but also for
attempts to generalize about the political connotations and effects of the
Methodist movement. It would further demonstrate the need for analyses
which differentiate as far as possible between the separate denominations, whatever the analysis being conducted. The systematic study of the
differences in social composition between denominations is as yet not far
advanced.[2] Too frequently in discussion of the effects of Methodism (its
influence on political or 'revolutionary' activity, on work discipline, on
organizational training, on domestic ideologies, on attitudes to welfare),
historians have treated the movement as a singular entity, making
generalizations which have largely ignored the substantial rifts between
the distinct sects involved.

There would probably be conspicuous question marks over an exercise
which compared the occupational structure of either of these two
Methodist groups with that of the Anglican Church. This is because the
degree of commitment which led to registration in an Anglican register
might differ from that which led a family to register a baptism, for example, in a Wesleyan or Primitive Methodist register. Anglican attendance
or registration was liable to have been influenced by local deferential
social relationships, particularly in rural areas, in a way that was less
common for Methodist registration, although this is a slippery matter
about which to speculate. However, in comparing different Methodist
denominations along these lines, issues like this are less problematic.
There is no very evident reason to suppose that the level of commitment
signalled by a registered vital event in a Wesleyan register was more or
less strong than that which led a family to register such an event within
the Primitive Methodist Church. And while a family might attend both
Anglican and one of the Methodist denominational services, it would
probably have been less common for a Wesleyan Methodist regularly to
attend also the services of a local Primitive Methodist chapel, and vice
versa. While one may have doubts about research which aimed to
contrast Anglican and Methodist occupational and class support, the
different Methodist registers themselves are much more acceptably
comparable.

Other difficulties might arise if one was to compare the occupational
differences between an older dissenting denomination, like the
Independents, with one of the Methodist sects. We have seen how the
Independents, Baptists, Quakers and Unitarians were more urban-located
than were the Wesleyan Methodists or Primitives. One would accordingly
expect the occupations of those entered in old dissenting registers to
differ from the more rural or small market-town occupations of the
Wesleyans, simply by virtue of the different rural and urban economic
sectors which provided the general contexts for the denominations. Some
'class' contrasts between these sects might well be expected and found,
but these could have been determined largely by the urban–rural
differences of emphasis already documented. However, as we have seen,

such problems will intrude less noticeably in the study of the occupational and social structure of the two main Methodist denominations because of their similar localisation, and for these reasons (as well as the need to explore the social adherence to denominations which were found to be regionally most closely located) this chapter will concentrate on the Primitive and Wesleyan Methodists.

Nineteenth-century baptism registers have been used to inquire into this issue of social difference between these denominations. The source has the advantage of indicating the occupation of the father at the point in his life which, in economic terms, may be felt most representative. It also covers a larger period of a man's life than do marriage or burial registers, and so is more likely to reflect accurately the composition of the male working population. Marriage and burial registers would prove less adequate as sources because they indicate occupations towards the start and end of a man's working life. Needless to say, it is almost impossible to examine these questions systematically for women. Baptism registers are evidently preferable to the use of occupational information for trustees, as the latter were only a small minority of believers, although information on them is illuminating for other questions.

Registers were taken for Leicestershire, Lincolnshire and Derbyshire.[3] A total of 7,273 baptisms providing a range of 482 recognizable male occupations were used, with no deflation of the total baptism figures to take account of fertility. In so far as one is concerned with a rudimentary comparison of the social structure of the two denominations, it was felt to be superfluous either to count separate fathers or to control for fertility, which might otherwise be necessary in a simple head count of this sort. It is unlikely that a method which analysed the occupations of fathers on an individual basis, rather than separate baptism basis, would yield significantly different results from those outlined here. During the period covered by these registers (1800–94) fertility differentials probably did not vary markedly between the two denominations, especially as the bulk of occupational detail refers to the period *c.* 1810–50, before the later nineteenth-century fertility decline. There is at present little detailed evidence on the existence of occupational fertility differences, or on demographic variation between different denominations. It is possible that marital fertility among a few of the occupational groups most sympathetic to the Primitives was relatively high. Fertility differentials between distinct occupations (consider for example the high fertility of miners indicated by the 1911 Census, or of other workers at that date in heavy labouring male-dominated workplaces) would in many cases have been offset by differential male mortality influenced by occupation, which may frequently be expected to have had the effect of minimizing differences in completed family size.[4]

It is known already that the Wesleyan Methodists were, as Currie put it, 'much the richest Methodists', that they had the lowest death rates among Methodists, and that the Primitives had the highest death rates.[5] As my earlier argument suggests, there were indeed noticeable occupational and class differences between these two Methodist denominations.

The Primitives emerge as considerably more proletarian than their Wesleyan Methodist counterparts. Labourers for example (very predominantly agricultural) comprised 28.8 per cent of the Primitives in these registers, but only 18.2 per cent of the Wesleyans. The various agricultural labouring occupations – adding to the field labourers such workmen as shepherds, castrators, carters, cottagers, gardeners, drovers, poultrymen, gamekeepers, and so on, but excluding farmers and all rural trades, shopkeepers, extractive and other workers – made up 31.3 per cent of the Primitives, and 20.7 per cent of the Wesleyans. In Lincolnshire they made up over half of the Primitives. In the whole region there were ten farm labourers to every one farmer among the Primitives; but the ratio was three to one among the Wesleyans.

The Primitive Methodists were of course to become intimately connected with the agricultural labour movement. As Gay expressed it: 'To a considerable extent Primitive Methodism was used by the 19th-century agricultural worker as a medium to fight his battle for recognition as a human being.'[6] The autobiographies of the agricultural union leaders and the studies of rural unionism make this abundantly clear.[7] 'Primitive Methodism was rural in its origin', wrote Kendall:

> it took kindly and naturally to the villages, and lingered amongst them lovingly. Village evangelisation became its habit – one might almost say its passion. . . . The need of the villages was our Church's opportunity, of which it was not slow to avail itself, and the effort to supply the need coincided entirely with the desires, the training, the habits, and the special qualifications of our missionaries, who, with scarce an exception, were village-born and village-bred. . . . Our Church did, by choice and preference, put its main strength into the work most urgently needed – the work of village evangelisation.[8]

The original occupations ascribed to the many early and mid-nineteenth-century Primitive Methodist preachers and leaders whose lives are outlined by Kendall bear out the same point: the most numerously recurring are labourer, shoemaker, farmer or 'cottage farmer', and framework-knitter.[9] In the parish returns for the 1851 Religious Census for Lincolnshire, the most commonly found occupations of preachers and officials of this Church were labourer, farmer, blacksmith, carpenter and grocer.[10]

Miners, colliers and workers in the various extractive industries made up 17.5 per cent of the Primitives and 2.1 per cent of the Wesleyans. There is abundant evidence of the rapport between colliers and Primitive Methodism. Kendall for example described the reaction of colliers confronted with the preaching of John Benton: 'Some groaned, others shrieked; some fell from their seats; and the whole assembly was thrown into consternation.'[11] Of 34 servants entered in the registers (including those who were female), all were Primitives. The Primitives in these registers had a near monopoly on the brickmakers, railway plate-layers, navvies, railway guards, railway porters or signalmen, tilemakers, fishermen, mariners, watermen, cottagers, shepherds, grooms, groundkeepers, sawyers, chimneysweeps, hawkers, shipwrights, boot and shoemakers, shoe hands (but not independent shoemakers, or cord-wainers, who were more evenly spread), nailers, miners and colliers, quarrymen, policemen, clerks, gasmen, or firemen. Transport, railway, sea, river and canal trades seem to have been heavily oriented towards the Primitives rather than the Wesleyan Methodists.

Framework-knitters comprised 11.7 per cent of the Primitives and 10.2 per cent of the Wesleyans: quite evenly spread between the two, but then this occupational term covered a wide range of workmen of differing skills, degrees of independence, earning capacity and status, working with different materials and producing products of very varied quality. The status of those engaged in the trade also changed markedly over time: the term suggested virtually the worst possible conditions of poverty in the Midlands by the 1840s.[12] Farmers on the other hand comprised 3.0 per cent of the Primitives and 7.0 per cent of the Wesleyans. For grocers and those who combined another trade with being a grocer, the respective percentages were 0.6 and 3.2; and it was much the same with millers. Higher status occupations were almost always Wesleyan Methodists rather than Primitives. Conspicuous examples were hosiers, worsted manufacturers, hairdressers, druggists, merchants, shopkeepers, haberdashers, marble-masons, carvers, cabinet-makers, coachbuilders, corn dealers, clock and watchmakers, cotton-spinners, drapers, excise officers, police superintendents, and surgeons.

There are commonplace problems in grouping these occupational data into social categories along the lines of the census social classes. From occupational designations *per se*, it is often hard to identify the appropriate class for placement. Furthermore, as with framework-knitting, the status and economic meaning of some occupational designations altered with skill-supplanting technologies or changes in wage differentials. It is almost impossible to take account of this. There has also been much debate over the appropriate social class categories which should be used for such an exercise.[13] This is not the place to dwell upon these issues or to discuss the exact criteria which underlie the picture provided by Table 10. The table gives the occupational data broken down into six social classes. The first of these is extraneous to these dissenters. Category II includes the usual professional occupations, and occupations such as 'manufacturer' (earthenware, cotton, worsted, cotton lace, lamb's wool, warp net), hosier, farmer, merchant, superintendent (of excise or police), or manager. Most of the many retail, tradesman, dealer, shopkeeper, food and drink occupations are in category III, alongside some lowly salaried workers, small administrators, clerks, salesmen, dissenting ministers, bailiffs, and the like. Category IV, skilled trades, comprises those involving productive processes in metalworking, textiles and clothing, wood, clay, leather and construction which traditionally involved an apprenticeship or extended period of training. This also includes some 'factory' workers. The semi-skilled group is formed by such workers as cratemakers, woodmen, gardeners, shoe hands, engine cleaners, checkweighmen, 'factory hands', railway plate-layers, or pointsmen. Finally, the 'unskilled' category covers

Table 10   Social structure of Wesleyan Methodists and Primitive Methodists in the North Midlands

Social Class	Primitives		Wesleyan Methodists	
	N	%	N	%
I Gentry	0	0.0	0	0.0
II Middle & professional	168	3.6	268	10.1
III Lower-middle	250	5.4	466	17.6
IV Skilled	1,289	27.9	1,086	41.0
V Semi-skilled	369	8.0	181	6.8
VI Unskilled	2,551	55.1	645	24.4
Total:	4,627	100	2,646	99.9

Source: Baptism registers for Leicestershire, Lincolnshire and Derbyshire. See note 3.

agricultural labourers, miners, porters, hawkers, coal heavers, navvies, cottagers, quarrymen and similar occupations, attention having been paid to analytical convention rather than to the abundant skills of some of these workers.

Conclusions emerge from table 10 which would not be called into question by the use of alternative categories. There is confirmation of conspicuous social differences between the two denominations. It is a striking finding that over half the male occupations entered in Primitive registers were unskilled, compared with a quarter for the Wesleyan Methodists. In fact, 91 per cent of all those baptised with the Primitives had fathers in categories IV, V and VI (skilled, semi-skilled and unskilled workers). Perhaps some of the Primitive Methodists represented in category IV would have been master artisans, or would no longer be working manually in their trade to the degree that might allow one to label them 'working-class' – but the same would be true for the Wesleyans, probably to a greater extent. Nevertheless, the overwhelming preponderance of Primitive Methodists were clearly manual workers or wage-dependent artisans with varied degrees of skill. The same would probably have been so for Wesleyan Methodists, but this was less striking as a feature of that denomination. Their constituency was more obviously drawn from the skilled working class, small artisan employers and the lower middle-class groups, with nevertheless a sizable number of unskilled workers.

The Wesleyan Methodists were not, however, dominated by the 'unskilled' manual workers. The very different denominationally-specific ratios between, for example, farmers and field labourers, tradespeople and colliers, signal the extent to which the Primitives had captured the allegiance of many who were socially inferior to the supposedly run-of-the-mill Wesleyan Methodists, who have so often given 'Methodism' a politically quiescent and upwardly mobile historiographical reputation. In some cases, certainly, Primitive Methodist success was in new regions for Methodism – notably in some Midland mining villages, in small coastal villages, and probably in some of the more isolated rural upland or fen areas. But the geographical picture suggested earlier of a denomination which spread Methodism downwards socially, rather than into new districts, is strongly supported by the occupational evidence in the registers. The corollary – given also the well-attested and often distinctive political and social beliefs of occupational groups like the field labourers, or the miners – was the development of differing social perspectives between regionally proximate Methodist sects as they absorbed the colour and occupational concerns of their followers. It is hard to imagine trade union meetings being regularly held in Wesleyan Methodist chapels, as they certainly were in the Primitives' places of worship.[14]

A further point ought to be stressed, however, on the issue of the regional association of types of Methodism. While there was a strong positive correlation between Wesleyan Methodism and the Primitives, showing their regional coincidence, the other Methodist denominations (taken together) were very weakly correlated with these two major Methodist sects. While not shown in the tables, the regional strength of the Wesleyans and the Primitives combined was negatively correlated in the north Midlands (using attendance data) with the remaining Methodist sects (−0.186), and statistically explained virtually none of their regionality. It seems that the positive correlation between the Wesleyans and the Primitives, and everything that it suggests in conjunction with occupational data about their social and regional orientations, did not obtain more generally within Methodism. The growth of the Methodist New Connexion, the Wesleyan Methodist Association, the Independent Methodists, the Wesleyan Reformers, and the Calvinistic Methodists of Lady Huntingdon's Connexion (when they are combined simply for the purpose of general analysis),[15] appears to have been only slightly influenced, and in a contrary direction to the Primitives, by the prior strength of the Wesleyan Church. A negative association (−0.295) obtained between the Wesleyan Methodists taken separately and these other Methodist sects, quite different from the association between the Wesleyans and the Primitives.

Much of the expansion of these other sects was therefore into new territory for the Methodists, away from the areas of Wesleyan consolidation and Primitive proletarian spread. To judge from the large numbers of farmers featured in the occasional New Connexion rural circuit register, this group may not have shared the more proletarian characteristics of the Primitives. Measured by 'attendance' data, these other sects were themselves negatively correlated with the Church of England (−0.354), indifferently correlated with the Primitives (0.059), the Baptists (−0.063) and the Independents (−0.146). At least when grouped together (and hence allowing for the possibility that one or more may be exceptions), they are best seen not as socially downward breakaway groups in particular areas from the Wesleyan Methodists, groups whose differing theological, political or social outlooks had nevertheless not led them to break new ground, but rather as sects which expanded into the interstices of Wesleyan strength, and most particularly into those areas where the Anglican Church was weak. It is significant that they did that to a greater extent than had the Wesleyan Methodists, when one considers the well-documented political and ostensibly democratic or even radical tenor of some of them. In so doing, it seems probable that they underwent less alteration in their social composition than had the Primitives as compared with the Wesleyans. The latter two denominations comprised the very large majority of Methodists, and future research will be able to determine the extent to which these two should be differentiated, as regionally proximate but with different social and ideological complexions, mirroring broader social divisions of Victorian society.

Chapter 6

The Southern Counties – Contrasts and Similarities

Consideration so far has been paid to the census of the North Midland counties, for the most part with as much denominational detail as was feasible given the methods used. I want now to extend coverage in a comparative way to the southern counties of Surrey, Kent, Sussex, Hampshire, Berkshire, Wiltshire, Dorset, Devon, Cornwall and Somerset, using the registration-district data prepared from the 1851 Census by Coleman.[1] The data for attendances (the index of attendance) was calculated by him in the same way as used here, although it was not initially corrected to deal with missing or inadequate census returns. For this reason it is not calculated on exactly the same principles as the North Midland data. Coleman grouped the returns together to form attendance figures only for the Anglican Church, the 'non-Anglican' denominations, old dissent, Methodism and Roman Catholicism. However, these group-ings will suffice to make general comparisons with the similar ones for the North Midlands. Coleman wished to map the registration-district 'index of attendance' (and attendances for each denominational grouping as a percentage of total attendances), so as to make descriptive statements about the religious characteristics of each southern county. He did not apply techniques like those used here. So it will be useful to apply such techniques to the southern counties to see whether conclusions on the North Midlands are representative of a more heavily Anglican dominated area. Given the broad denominational groupings, it is not likely that the failure to correct the southern census figures vitiates the basis for comparison. While some caution is called for, one doubts that the results will thereby be very significantly altered.

Table 11 shows the overall correlation coefficients for the southern figures. A number of conclusions stand out. The most notable is that 'Methodism' was inversely correlated with the Anglican Church, as well as being inversely associated, to a lesser degree, with old dissent. The latter was weakly but positively correlated with the Church of England. Roman Catholicism, omitted from the discussion of the North Midlands, was not significantly related to any of the other three groups, but it can

Table 11 Correlation coefficients between denominational groupings for the 174 registration districts of Surrey (extra-metropolitan), Kent (extra-metropolitan), Sussex, Hampshire, Berkshire, Wiltshire, Dorset, Devon, Cornwall and Somerset

	Anglican	*Non-Anglican*	*Old Dissent*	*Methodism*
Anglican				
Non-Anglican	−0.268			
Old Dissent	0.151	0.522		
Methodism	−0.407	0.740	−0.164	
Roman Catholic	−0.080	0.020	0.019	−0.071

Source: Computed from Index of Attendance data in B.I. Coleman, 'Southern England in the Religious Census of 1851', *Southern History*, 5 (1983), 183–7.

readily be shown in the south and the North Midlands that it was most marked in areas of high population because of the Irish presence in urban areas. (It was also to be found in the North Midlands in places like Hassop, Glossop, Ecklington and Hathersage, where recusant families such as the Howards were major landowners.) Comparison of table 11 with table 7 suggests very similar overall patterns. The association between the Anglican Church and all Methodism was virtually identical (−0.407 and −0.406); and the relation between old dissent and the Anglican Church, and between Methodism and old dissent were similar to the southern pattern in the North Midlands, although the correlations were noticeably more pronounced.

The reasons for this with regard to Methodism and old dissent would probably have to be sought in the more industrial and scattered settlement patterns of parts of the North Midlands, with the key being the marked tendency for Methodism to become strongly established in areas often remote from the existing centres of old dissent, which themselves happened to concur relatively weakly with areas of Anglican strength. The North Midlands correlations of table 7 suggested that in seeking an answer to the location of Methodism in that region, one should pay more heed to the prior strength of old dissent, than to that of the Church of England. In the southern counties the opposite was true: there Methodism was much more evidently filling the gaps of the established church, rather than the areas where old dissent was weak. The social and economic dominance of the Church of England in the south might lead one to expect this. However, it should be stressed that while the relationship between Methodism and the Church of England remains statistically the same in the North Midlands, the overriding consideration here affecting the location of Methodism was the situation of old dissent.

These points can be shown most clearly by looking at the coefficients of determination between these three denominational groups. This statistic shows what proportion of the variation in one variable is 'explained' by the influence of the other. Table 12 gives these (expressed as percentages) so that the comparisons between the south and the North Midlands can immediately be realized. In the southern counties, Anglican strength explained 16.6 per cent of the geographical variance of the

Table 12 Coefficients of determination between the Anglican Church, Old
Dissent and Methodism, for southern counties and the North Midlands
(attendances data).

	Southern counties	North Midlands
Church of England & Old Dissent	2.3%	12.1%
Church of England & Methodism	16.6%	16.5%
Old Dissent & Methodism	2.7%	33.8%

figures for Methodism – almost identical to the North Midlands. But while
Anglican strength explained only about 2 per cent of the variance of old
dissent in the south, in the North Midlands it explained about 12 per cent.
And while in the south old dissent explained only 2.7 per cent of the
variance in Methodism, in the North Midlands it explained as much as 33.8
per cent. The comparison is intriguing, and demonstrates the extent to
which historiographical generalizations on these issues ought to be
modified to take account of regional differences. There is little doubt that
this point would be reinforced still further by considering regions north of
any treated here, or Wales, or the West Midlands or East Anglia.

Table 13 Southern county correlation coefficients between the Anglican Church,
Old Dissent and Methodism.

County	Anglican & Old Dissent	Anglican & Methodism	Old Dissent & Methodism
Surrey	−0.595	0.659	−0.596
Kent	−0.118	0.139	−0.222
Sussex	−0.206	−0.469	0.263
Hampshire	0.073	0.287	0.045
Berkshire	−0.050	0.016	−0.302
Wiltshire	−0.248	−0.298	−0.124
Dorset	−0.389	−0.284	−0.048
Devon	0.451	−0.280	−0.349
Cornwall	0.028	0.018	−0.361
Somerset	0.187	−0.614	0.031

Source: As for table 11.

Such differences were also apparent between the southern counties
themselves, as can be seen in table 13. The counties show considerable
variations. Some of the results demand further analysis, as for example
the lack of any correlation between the Anglican Church and Methodism
in Cornwall, which is contrary to expectation, or the clear-cut relationships in Surrey. These areas await further examination. One thing is
clear, however: one could not argue from these figures that certain types
of association apply generally to all counties. In some cases the numbers
of registration districts per county are quite small. And no doubt there
has been some blurring of results by the bringing together of sects into
'Methodism' and 'old dissent'. Further, one doubts that the uncorrected

southern census data used here are themselves sufficiently accurate and rigorous to render highly significant results, even if the reality of nineteenth-century religious geography warranted this. Despite such thoughts, however, one is most struck here, as in the North Midlands, by the variety between counties and the contrasting situation in each. Even proximate counties show varied results. In so far as generalizations can be made from registration-district data about which denominational strengths and weaknesses coincided, they commonly have to be made by grouping the registration districts of a number of counties together to form general census-type regions. One should stress, however, that in the south as in the North Midlands, such generalizations will often be contrary to individual county patterns within the overall region.

Chapter 7

Conclusion

I hope to have demonstrated how methods used in the study of religious local history might be diversified by more fully incorporating other approaches. The subject can clearly be 'known' in many different ways, and the questions posed of it may be answered, and even raised, in ways which go beyond the possibilities currently realized. No single approach to the subject is complete in itself. The close reliance upon appropriate literary evidence should continue to be the main focus for research – no claim is being made here that a quantitative approach to the local history of religion should have primacy. It has been rightly observed by one historian of religion in the Midlands that behind all the statistics 'are the now-shadowy figures of ordinary men, women and children with their problems, beliefs and aspirations, responding each in his or her own way to the zeal and fervour of the dissenting evangelists';[1] and due attention must continue to be paid to the fascinating social and subjective elements of religious appeal.

Yet as a way of refining current knowledge, and as an opening to more thorough comparative approaches, I hope that the advantages of quantitative methods are evident. Those methods themselves are advancing rapidly, particularly with developments in computerized analytical mapping facilities. More exhaustive investigations are now in progress which encompass the whole of England and Wales, computing all the (reworked) registration-district data of the Religious Census, while analysis is being extended to the settlement-level data of the Compton Census, the 1829 religious returns and the 1851 Religious Census, developing some of the approaches suggested here.[2] This will set up an overall pattern against which the experiences of different regions will be tested and compared. It will enable far closer inspection of continuities over time in regional religious behaviour. It will throw further light onto those aspects of nineteenth-century society which were associated with different religious configurations, incorporating in the analysis other social, economic and perhaps political variables. Such research will locate more accurately those features which were hostile to any form of religion, thus addressing one of the key historical questions of the modern period. It will consider areas with distinctive religious experiences, as defined by patterns in the data, working towards a more thorough interpretation of cultural regions and religious pluralism.

For the kind of analysis undertaken on this occasion, it is possible that the registration district is slightly too large a unit, although it is of course a much more viable choice than the more commonly used county area. Nor perhaps does the unit used do justice to the particular experiences of various types of towns, especially market towns, themselves located in different *pays*, given that urban boundaries were often blurred by the administrative requirements of registration districts largely identical with poor-law unions. Registration districts were of very varied sizes, and they did not always respect the conventional county boundaries. As units, they comprised the whole spectrum of the urban–rural mix, although for some kinds of analysis this is a matter which can be partly overcome by 'urbanization' or 'ruralization' measures, such as those used.

Alternatively, the parish by itself may sometimes be too small for comprehensive analysis along such lines. The question of the sorts of parish which fostered dissent is intriguing, and Everitt has shown where one would most expect to find dissenting chapels.[3] However, for my purposes, the crucial matter is the local availability of viable places of worship and the demand for them. Chapels were often deliberately built to cater for more than one parish, and the parish boundary was often meaningless in such situations. Dissenters very commonly crossed parochial boundaries to worship, like many of their circuit preachers even walking long distances. The absence of a chapel within their immediate parish, township or hamlet of residence would not generally have proved a major obstacle to the exercise of their choice of worship. The extent of extra-parochial baptism also indicates this.

Much dissent was a denial of the conventional sense of place, a denial of everything the Anglican Church stood for in local/parochial political and social terms. Thus the local area and coverage appropriate to one denomination could differ markedly from that of another; and the units historians might conceive for analysis were not experienced in the same way by people of different sectarian loyalties, posing problems for the comparison of denominations. This comparative denominational sense of place, and the many political and social connotations of it, awaits further study, relating it to broader issues of social relationships, administration, occupational community, settlement, and socially contrasting cultural regions.

Joseph Ashby went to church on Sunday mornings 'but claimed freedom to wander in the evenings, visiting the "Primitive" and "Wesleyan" chapels in Tysoe and sometimes going off across the fields to chapels and churches in other villages'.[4] Others had less choice in their own parish. The characteristics associated with a so-called 'close' or landlord-dominated parish would usually have militated against chapel-building; but recourse could always be had to the more variegated 'open' parish nearby, perhaps after routine attendance at the morning Anglican service of one's home parish.[5] Something of the same would have remained true of the majority of parishes ranging between those with very marked 'open' or 'close' characteristics. The development of such separations of parish type, in so far as these terms were being used in the mid-nineteenth century, was mainly influenced by poor-law and labour-market considerations, and so was virtually always dependent upon the possibility of labourers walking daily between them.[6] This was a society in which the everyday walking of long distances was taken for granted, as one knows from *Lark Rise to Candleford* and so much other literary and autobiographical material.[7] For quantitative purposes the historian requires regional units which allow for this practice of cross-parochial mobility for worship. The poor-law union was adequate for the peripatetic relieving officer, and perforce had to be adequate for the frequently unfit parish pauper hoping to be presented to the Board of Guardians. Accordingly, and in the absence of more appropriate districts, it may be best suited to analysis of the kind used here.

Ideally, however, such analysis – while invaluable in qualifying generalizations based upon county distinctions over the whole of England and Wales – needs itself to be supplemented by use of parish-specific data from the enumerators' books, looking at particular counties or areas within them and grouping data accordingly. The much lower figures involved (for example, of places of worship) may make correlation less practicable as a tool; and one faces problems in relating attendance figures to population size when so many moved for worship. However, simpler ranking or relational methods can be used.[8] Of the many generalizations current in religious historiography which lend themselves to statistical verification, it will then be possible to see which stand up at county, *pays*, registration-district, parish or township level, and to refine them accordingly. The differing pictures emerging would lend themselves to a closer understanding of the scale of regional patterns of interdenominational location in the mid-nineteenth century, of the sense of religious space demanded, and so to a better appreciation of the local social effects of denominational dispersal.

As Mann pointed out, the question of the reasons for the location of different denominations is of considerable interest in its own right. It also has an important bearing on the interpretation of regional cultural differences in the past, a matter which has not preoccupied me here. Beyond such issues, and beyond advancing understanding of how certain denominations like the Primitives and Bible Christians (or old and new dissent generally) complemented each other regionally,[9] one of the advantages of the approach advocated is to provide a precisely drawn background and context against which to understand interdenominational rivalry and conflict. For the laying-down of statistical interdenominational relationships, and geographical patterns, bears on many other debates in religious historiography, debates which might not at first sight seem amenable to a quantitative contribution, but which have all too often taken place with no reference to geographical context and local territorial prerogatives. A statistical relationship on the ground between two or more denominations is obviously a different matter to a social, theological or political relationship. Nobody would wish to deduce the latter in any simple manner from the former. Yet the two are certainly connected and influence each other in a variety of ways, and an advantage of the methods used here is that they help to define problems and historical possibilities which can then be resolved by time-honoured but perhaps more subtle use of literary evidence.

For example, if Wesleyan Methodism did indeed generally grow in areas of weak Anglicanism, filling vacuums left by Anglican laxity or absence, the conclusions regarding the political stance of Wesleyan membership, or even of the Conference, will be different from those drawn if the denomination grew strong in local Anglican ministers' back gardens. The potential for continuing face-to-face conflict in the latter situation was immediate, although it could be variously resolved by local or national compromises in Wesleyan ideology, of the sort which are often discussed.[10] In the former case, growing in areas of weak Anglicanism, the chance of conflict was more remote, and Wesleyan Methodism or the Primitives were the more readily tolerated or ignored by representatives of the established church. Gilbert touched on this issue, discussing the contrast between areas of weak or assertive Anglican control:

> It meant that relations between Church and Chapel tended to be far more strained in the south and the south-east than in those areas where the parochial system was weakest. The element of *conscious* dissent was not necessarily present in the huge destitute areas of the north-east, for example. There was often nothing to dissent from. But in that belt of counties stretching from Dorset to Wiltshire, through the south Midlands, into East Anglia, which the 1851 Religious Census would discover to have the highest overall rates of religious practice in England, the relatively close proximity of church and Chapel strongholds produced competition, acrimony and sometimes considerable Establishment harassment of Nonconformists.[11]

This regional reaction of the established church is quite well documented. Yet one can also note the possibility that if (or where) Wesleyan expansion was in or very proximate to areas of Anglican strength – south and mid-Nottinghamshire, for example – then its official local standpoints might necessarily have been more conciliatory, more conservative, than in other counties such as north Lincolnshire. In an area like Nottinghamshire its position (as perceived by many local clergymen, justices of the peace and landowners) had after all been the more open to attack as a threat rather than a reinforcement to the political and ecclesiastical establishment in periods of political agitation and suspicion, such as the wartime and anti-Jacobite years of the 1740s, or during the Napoleonic Wars. The relation between the Anglican and Methodist churches, and the positions they took up with regard to each other, were probably more regionally varied than some mainstream debates have made out, and (unlike the regional understanding of parallel issues which has been emerging for the seventeenth century) there has been little attempt to make sense of the conflicting localized evidence of mutual compatibility or downright hostility.[12] Precise statistical descriptions of denominational regional strengths and complementary location should make the basis for such variation more apparent, and allow the conflicts which developed or remained muted to be better understood.

Wesley's own projected and conservative image of his movement was one which could best be sustained in those areas where Methodism did indeed fill in for the absence of the established church. It was of course in his own interests to stress this. From its earliest days, Wesleyan evangelizing had also to be placatory to the interests of the established church: Wesley himself had laid greatest stress on his efforts in the supposedly outlandish outposts of the mining, fishing or other industrial villages, and these certainly provide some of the most prominent scenarios in his *Journal*. A tendency to generalize from striking and well-documented examples of mass conversion in such areas has been a feature of much Methodist historiography since. There is no doubt that in many disparate and often remote rural, coastal and newly industrial parishes chapels were built to supply the lack of churches. This is true in the Fens, in the Forest of Dean, in upland parts of Derbyshire, in Headington, Leeds, Halifax, Sheffield and many other such places. We have seen that one of the advantages of a quantitative approach is to keep such examples in proportion and not to lose sight of the overall coverage of the distinct Methodist sects in regions where they were stronger if perhaps more mundane or orthodox in their psychological impact, regions indeed where Methodist political positions were much more likely to have been fostered and to have had wider significance.

A further advantage of quantification is that the relative influence upon Methodism of the Anglican Church and of old dissent can be weighed, with a precision which otherwise eludes us. It appears for many areas of the North Midlands, at any rate, that a proximate situation of Wesleyan Methodism to the Church of England could overshadow those cases where it evangelized outposts of early industrial society poorly catered for by the established church. And variation in Anglican strength could exercise a surprisingly weak influence upon Methodist growth. Over the whole region, certain counties aside, it was indeed the case that 'Methodism' in general was negatively correlated with the Anglican Church. However, for this region, to a much greater extent than appeared true further south, it seems that the thesis which Tillyard advanced, and himself failed to demonstrate, was true and ought to be highlighted. It is now clear that much further research should be directed at that neglected juncture within the religious triad: at the relationships between varieties of Methodism and forms of old dissent.[13] For in the North Midlands it was the distribution of the latter, rather than of the Anglican Church, which exerted by far the strongest influence upon the regional growth of Methodism. We need to know how and why, through what manner of reciprocities and understandings, this came about.

Appendix A

Percentage of population present at the most numerously attended services, England and Wales, 30/3/1851

	County	Church of England	Protestant Dissenters
A	Middlesex (part of)	11.3	7.9
	Surrey (part of)	12.0	7.3
	Kent (part of)	15.8	9.8
B	Surrey (extra-Metrop.)	23.5	7.4
	Kent (extra-Metrop.)	22.4	13.3
	Sussex	22.6	11.0
	Hampshire	23.1	15.9
	Berkshire	21.2	13.5
C	Middlesex (extra-Metrop.)	19.7	9.5
	Hertfordshire	24.8	19.1
	Buckinghamshire	26.0	22.1
	Oxfordshire	26.4	15.3
	Northamptonshire	26.5	21.7
	Huntingdonshire	27.3	27.7
	Bedfordshire	24.0	32.6
	Cambridgeshire	25.6	20.4
D	Essex	22.1	19.8
	Suffolk	30.0	19.1
	Norfolk	23.2	17.2
E	Wiltshire	26.4	23.9
	Dorset	30.1	16.3
	Devon	22.6	17.2
	Cornwall	12.6	32.5
	Somerset	25.5	17.6
F	Gloucestershire	21.2	18.3
	Herefordshire	21.8	9.8
	Shropshire	22.5	15.9

Contd.

	County	Church of England	Protestant Dissenters
	Staffordshire	13.2	17.1
	Worcestershire	20.1	11.1
	Warwickshire	15.8	11.3
G	Leicestershire	21.7	23.1
	Rutland	28.2	18.6
	Lincolnshire	18.4	22.6
	Nottinghamshire	15.9	21.1
	Derbyshire	14.3	23.4
H	Cheshire	14.5	16.1
	Lancashire	10.8	10.9
I	West Riding	10.4	20.4
	East Riding (with York)	15.2	21.9
	North Riding	19.5	23.5
J	Durham	9.2	15.8
	Northumberland	9.7	16.2
	Cumberland	13.7	10.3
	Westmorland	20.7	11.6
K	Monmouthshire	13.2	30.4
	South Wales	10.0	36.4
	North Wales	9.8	42.9

Source: 1851 Census of Religious Worship.

Appendix B

The North Midlands: Places of Worship, Sittings and Attendants for each Denomination

Total population: 1,214,538	Number of places of worship and sittings		Number of attendants at public worship on Sunday, 30 March 1851		
Religious denominations	Places of worship	Sittings	Morning	Afternoon	Evening
TOTAL	3,627	787,837	273,406	250,682	241,917
Protestant Churches:					
Church of England	1,499	395,003	154,357	137,250	49,205
Independents	157	47,742	20,565	10,333	16,030
Baptists:					
General Baptists	39	5,791	224	2,763	2,370
Particular Baptists	77	20,952	9,118	4,860	8,516
Scotch Baptists	1	350	–	220	178
General Baptist New Connexion	119	33,682	13,470	7,682	17,599
Baptists (undefined)	21	4,350	1,411	1,356	1,890
Society of Friends	22	4,197	550	266	70
Unitarians	20	4,809	1,672	239	943
Moravians	1	227	141	110	150
Wesleyan Methodists:					
Original Connexion	963	169,706	41,745	49,398	80,163
New Connexion	30	8,884	3,615	2,049	4,980
Primitive Methodists	470	59,268	9,491	26,022	40,673
Wesleyan Methodist Association	25	4,263	1,649	1,004	2,582
Independent Methodists	5	580	–	290	299
Wesleyan Reformers	66	11,539	4,791	2,720	8,355
Calvinist Methodists:					
Lady Huntingdon's Connexion	4	860	368	218	297
New Church	4	685	291	–	239

Contd.

Total population: 1,214,538	Number of places of worship and sittings		Number of attendants at public worship on Sunday, 30 March 1851		
Religious denominations	*Places of worship*	*Sittings*	*Morning*	*Afternoon*	*Evening*
Isolated Congregations	33	3,877	1,576	660	1,861
Other Christian Churches					
Roman Catholics	39	8,030	8,020	2,131	3,542
Catholic and Apostolic Church	1	400	–	–	–
Latter Day Saints, or Mormons	30	2,592	325	1,096	1,961
Jews	1	50	27	15	14

Source: 1851 Census of Religious Worship, p. cxc.

Appendix C

Total North Midlands Attendances for each Denomination as a Percentage of each Registration-District Population: the 'index of attendances'

	Church of England	Wesleyan Methodists	Primitive Methodists	Baptists	Independents
Leics. & Rutland					
Lutterworth	47.2	0.8	1.1	9.2	16.1
Market Harborough	57.7	5.3	0.0	11.0	21.7
Billesdon	47.2	13.3	0.5	3.6	2.6
Blaby	43.3	4.7	4.5	13.2	19.4
Hinckley	35.7	15.8	3.6	9.1	13.5
Market Bosworth	47.0	10.1	7.6	18.7	0.9
Ashby-de-la-Zouch	40.1	12.4	5.3	11.8	0.9
Loughborough	31.1	13.3	4.3	19.3	2.2
Barrow upon Soar	30.5	12.2	13.5	13.6	0.0
Leicester	35.9	2.7	3.0	14.6	4.8
Melton Mowbray	52.3	22.6	4.7	2.2	4.0
Oakham } Rutland	50.6	12.3	2.0	11.0	3.2
Uppingham }	48.8	7.5	0.0	9.5	7.0
Lincs.					
Stamford	48.7	6.7	0.3	2.9	4.6
Bourne	32.4	9.0	0.6	5.9	3.8
Spalding	33.9	12.3	6.0	9.0	3.7
Holbeach	25.8	17.3	7.3	12.6	3.4
Boston	26.5	18.2	3.6	5.8	2.9
Sleaford	28.8	18.1	5.0	2.6	6.1
Grantham	45.2	8.5	3.9	0.9	3.0
Lincoln	32.7	24.7	4.6	1.4	2.6
Horncastle	28.5	31.1	7.6	1.9	1.5
Spilsby	33.9	26.7	3.8	2.2	1.4
Louth	27.6	25.4	11.7	4.9	1.0
Caistor	27.5	26.5	11.9	1.8	1.0
Glanford Brigg	26.7	23.0	15.7	1.7	3.3

contd.

	Church of England	Wesleyan Methodists	Primitive Methodists	Baptists	Independents
Gainsborough	26.1	24.8	20.9	0.3	2.0
Notts.					
East Retford	29.1	20.1	2.9	1.9	2.1
Worksop	30.3	10.1	0.9	0.0	1.7
Mansfield	28.9	9.5	6.0	5.2	5.3
Basford	19.8	9.5	6.5	10.3	2.1
Radford	11.2	3.7	2.5	1.0	1.7
Nottingham	19.2	7.1	5.3	8.8	6.2
Southwell	41.6	16.7	8.5	2.3	0.4
Newark	34.8	23.7	3.2	4.1	3.0
Bingham	41.5	25.3	12.5	0.2	2.1
Derby.					
Shardlow	33.9	15.8	6.7	8.4	2.4
Derby	28.3	5.0	4.5	7.2	5.2
Belper	24.4	14.8	10.2	9.2	4.4
Ashbourne	38.1	9.6	14.4	0.5	1.8
Chesterfield	19.9	9.9	7.6	1.0	3.4
Bakewell	26.5	15.0	12.8	0.4	5.7
Chapel-en-le-Frith	22.8	22.4	6.0	0.4	1.1
Hayfield	15.3	19.1	6.4	1.2	10.4

Source: 1851 Census of Religious Worship, corrected for missing returns.

Notes

Chapter 1. *Quantification and Religious Historiography*

I am grateful to Paul Ell, Charles Phythian-Adams, David Thompson, Margery Tranter and David Wykes for their helpful comments.

1. J.D. Gay, *The Geography of Religion in England* (1971), p. 22.
2. One thinks in particular here of R. Currie, A. Gilbert and L. Horsley, *Churches and Churchgoers. Patterns of Church Growth in the British Isles since 1700* (Oxford, 1977); J.D. Gay, *The Geography of Religion in England* (1971); R. Currie, *Methodism Divided: a Study in the Sociology of Ecumenicalism* (1968); A.D. Gilbert, *Religion and Society in Industrial England: Church, Chapel and Social Change, 1740–1914* (1976); and A. Everitt, *The Pattern of Rural Dissent: the Nineteenth Century* (Leicester, 1972); H. McLeod, *Class and Religion in the Late Victorian City* (1974); N. Yates, 'Urban church attendance and the use of statistical evidence, 1850–1900', in D. Baker (ed.), *Studies in Church History, 16: The Church in Town and Countryside* (Oxford, 1979). However, none of these authors provides analysis in the terms used here. R.A. Soloway in 1972 commented upon 'the increase of scholars generalizing about religious behaviour on the basis of quantifiable evidence – particularly that provided by the unique national religious census of 1851', but for the most part this has not yet developed into any significant analytical advance. His statement that 'much work remains' to be done with the 1851 census and the numerous ecclesiastical visitation returns is still true. See his 'Church and society. Recent trends in nineteenth-century religious history', *Journal of British Studies*, 11 (1972), 152. For figures on twentieth-century religious patterns, see in particular the editions of *Social Trends*, and R. Currie and A. Gilbert, 'Religion', in A.H. Halsey (ed.), *Trends in British Society since 1900* (1972), pp. 407–50.
3. See e.g. The summary given in Gilbert, *Religion and Society in Industrial England* pp. 59–67; H. McLeod, *Religion and the Working Class in Nineteenth-century Britain* (1984), p. 24, and the references there; H. McLeod, *Class and Religion in the Late Victorian City* (1974), pp. 309–11; H. Perkin, *The Origins of Modern English Society, 1780–1880* (1969, 1976 edn), pp. 196–207; M.R. Watts, *The Dissenters from the Reformation to the French Revolution* (Oxford, 1978); J.S. Werner, *The Primitive Methodist Connexion: its Background and Early History* (1984), pp. 25, 83, 122; D. Hempton, *Methodism and Politics in British Society. 1750–1850* (1984, 1987 edn), p. 14; C.D. Field, 'The social structure of English Methodism:

eighteenth–twentieth centuries', *British Journal of Sociology*, 28 (1977); J. Foster, *Class Struggle and the Industrial Revolution: Early Industrial Capitalism in Three English Towns* (1974, 1979 edn), pp. 168, 215.

4. The work of Michael Watts, and other research by Tony Wrigley, on occupations from different denominational registers, will enhance understanding of these issues, as well as shedding light on more general shifts in the occupational structure before the detailed occupational censuses.

5. H. Mann, 'On the statistical position of religious bodies in England and Wales', *Journal of the Statistical Society*, XVIII (1855), 155.

6. This is most notably the case in A. Everitt's pioneering work. See in particular his *The Pattern of Rural Dissent: the Nineteenth Century* (Leicester, 1972). See also his 'Nonconformity in country parishes', in J. Thirsk (ed.), *Land, Church and People. Essays Presented to H.P.R. Finberg* (Reading, 1970). For further discussion of the parochial variations in religious adherence, see D. Mills, 'English villages in the eighteenth and nineteenth centuries: a sociological approach', *Amateur Historian*, VI (1963–5), 277; D.M. Thompson, 'The churches and society in nineteenth-century rural England: a rural perspective', in G.J. Cuming and D. Baker (eds), *Studies in Church History, 8: Popular Practice and Belief* (Cambridge, 1972), pp. 267–76; M. Tranter, Aspects of the Development of Dissent in Rural Derbyshire, 1662–1851 (M.A. Dissertation, University of Leicester, 1974); and her 'Landlords, labourers, local preachers: rural nonconformity in Derbyshire, 1772–1851', *Derbyshire Archaeological Journal*, 101 (1981), 119–38; D.G. Hey, 'The pattern of Nonconformity in South Yorkshire, 1660–1851', *Northern History*, 8 (1973), 86–118; C.P. Griffin, 'Methodism in the Leicestershire and South Derbyshire coalfield', *Proceedings of the Wesley Historical Society*, 39 (1973), 62–72.

7. F. Tillyard, 'The distribution of the Free Churches in England', *Sociological Review*, XXVII (1935), 1–18.

8. *Ibid.*, 11. His figures unfortunately did not do justice to those denominations which relied heavily upon non-stipendiary lay preachers.

9. This method is much used throughout this discussion. In interpreting the results of correlation, we may remind ourselves that correlation coefficients can range between -1 and $+1$: a negative coefficient demonstrates an inverse relationship between the two variables concerned, and a positive one indicates that the two denominations in question are positively correlated – that is, for each case they are either both strong, or both weak, in conjunction with the other. A result of zero (or approaching zero) indicates a lack of correlation between the two denominations in question. A value of $+1$ indicates perfect positive correlation, and -1 perfect negative correlation. To a limited extent, the method was also used by Currie *et al.*, *Churches and Churchgoers*, e.g. pp. 87, 94; and by McLeod, *Class and Religion in the Late Victorian City*, e.g. pp. 299–303, 315–16. Accounts of correlation and regression will be found in R. Floud, *An Introduction to Quantitative Methods for Historians* (1973, 1974 edn), pp. 138–54; V. Liveanu *et al.*, 'Coefficients of correlation in historical research', in F.R. Hodson, D.G. Kendall and P. Tautu (eds), *Mathematics in the Archaeological and Historical Sciences* (Edinburgh, 1971), pp. 505–15; R.G.D. Allen, *Statistics for Economists* (1949, 1972 edn), chapter 7; D. Ebdon, *Statistics in Geography* (Oxford, 1977, 1978 edn), pp. 74–105; H.M. Blalock, *Social Statistics* (1960, 1972 edn), chapters 17, 18, 19; R.A. Cooper and A.J. Weekes, *Data, Models and Statistical Analysis* (1983), pp. 9–11, 180–259. Most statistics textbooks in economics, social science, geography or business studies have a chapter or more on this subject.

10. R. Currie, 'A micro-theory of Methodist growth', *Proceedings of the Wesleyan Historical Society*, XXXVI (1967), 68.

11. His valuable book is rare in its use of outline statistics: A.D. Gilbert, *Religion*

and Society in Industrial England, p. 94. See also the interesting historiographical essay by H. McLeod, *Religion and the Working Class in Nineteenth-Century Britain* (1984), p. 22:

> It is common ground that chapels sprang up where the Established Churches were weak: in new communities without their own parish church, in outlying hamlets, in working-class neighbourhoods of cities. It is evident that groups such as the Methodists were filling a vacuum left by the failure of the Established Churches.
>
> To similar effect see J. Gay, *Geography of Religion*, pp. 109, 145, 147–8, 159:
>
> > The distribution pattern of Methodism which emerged in the 19th century was largely determined by the geographical variations in the Church of England's ability to maintain a proper pastoral oversight of the people in the 18th century. As a faithful member of the Church of England John Wesley saw his own work as complementing and reinforcing the work of the Established Church in areas where the Church was weak. Where the Church was running efficiently and catering for the needs of the local community, Wesley left well alone. . . . Methodism was to become most influential in the areas where the Church of England had failed to provide for the pastoral needs of the people – in Cornwall, the Black Country, the north-east and the new industrial areas in Lancashire and Yorkshire.

12. Gilbert, *Religion and Society in Industrial England*, p. 110.
13. Everitt, *The Pattern of Rural Dissent*.
14. C. Kingsley, *Yeast* (1851, 1902 edn), p. 90.
15. B.I. Coleman, *The Church of England in the Mid-Nineteenth Century: A Social Geography* (1980), p. 9. See also his 'Southern England in the Census of Religious Worship, 1851', *Southern History*, 5 (1983).
16. Gilbert, *Religion and Society in Industrial England*, e.g. pp. 109–20. See also his chapter 5: 'The pattern of Nonconformist encroachment'.

Chapter 2. The 1851 Religious Census: Problems and Possibilities

1. K.S. Inglis, 'Patterns of religious worship in 1851', *Journal of Ecclesiastical History*, II (1960), 79. See also R.W. Ambler (ed.), Lincolnshire Returns of the Census of Religious Worship, 1851, *Lincoln Record Society*. 72 (1979), p. xxii: 'It was taken conscientiously and with a fair degree of general accuracy, a verdict which is confirmed by other investigations'; D.M. Thompson, 'The Religious Census of 1851', in R. Lawton (ed.), *The Census and Social Structure: an Interpretative Guide to Nineteenth-century Censuses for England and Wales* (1978), p. 248: its 'completeness is impressive'.
2. For detailed discussion of the merits and shortcomings of the Religious Census, see Mann, 'On the statistical position of religious bodies in England and Wales'; Inglis, 'Patterns of religious worship in 1851'; W.S.F. Pickering, 'The 1851 Religious Census – a useless experiment?', *British Journal of Sociology*, 18 (1967), 382–407; D. Thompson, 'The Religious Census: problems and possibilities', *Victorian Studies*, II (1967), 87–97); and in particular his 'The Religious Census of 1851', in R. Lawton (ed.), *The Census and Social Structure* (1978); J. Rogan, 'The Religious Census of 1851', *Theology* (1963), 11–15; Gay, *The Geography of Religion in England*, pp. 45–63; R.M. Goodridge, 'The religious condition of the West Country in 1851', *Social Compass*, XIV (1967), 285–96; R.W. Ambler (ed.), Lincolnshire Returns (1979), introduction; and his 'The 1851 Census of Religious Worship', *The Local Historian*, 11 (1975), 375–81; D.W. Bushby (ed.), Bedfordshire Ecclesiastical Census, 1851, in *Bedfordshire Historical Record Society*, 54 (1975); I.G. Jones and D. Williams (eds), *The*

Religious Census of 1851. A Calendar of the Returns Relating to Wales. Vol. 1. South Wales (Cardiff, 1976). Except where they obviously may affect the argument and the statistics calculated, I shall not reiterate the cautionary points made by these authors on the Religious Census. Some other matters regarding the use of the Census which have largely been overlooked, and other ways of testing its reliability, will be treated here.

3. See A. Mearns (ed.), *The Statistics of Attendance at Public Worship, as Published by the Local Press, 1881–2* (1882); R. Mudie-Smith (ed.), *The Religious Life of London* (1904). On the 1829 returns, which frequently do not survive, see R.W. Ambler, 'Religious life in Kesteven – a return of the number of places of worship not of the Church of England, 1829', *Lincolnshire History and Archaeology*, 220 (1985), 59–64; his 'A lost source? The 1829 returns of non-Anglican places of worship', *Local Historian* (1987); N. Caplan, 'Sussex religious dissent, *c.* 1830', *Sussex Archaeological Collections*, 120 (1982), 193–203. For discussion of the possibilities of the Compton Census, see A. Whiteman (ed.), *The Compton Census of 1676: A Critical Edition*, Records of Social and Economic History, New Series, vol, X (Oxford, 1986).

4. Correlation using the fourth measure (the percentage share for each denomination of total attendances) will of course almost always produce negative results, especially for the larger denominations, because of the way in which the figures are calculated – and so it should generally be avoided. This objection does not hold for the other calculations possible. Some of these other figures use a common denominator (the registration-district population), and so cannot be completely independent of each other. Yet that denominator is being used to contrast the actual attendances, or sittings, and it is essentially the respective numbers of these which are being displayed. There seems to be no other feasible way to calculate the figures, and it would evidently be dubious to correlate without controlling for registration-district population. Population size by itself, without regard to density, is unlikely to have been a major explanatory variable. Correlation using ratios with a common denominator is common in economic and social research. In regression the use of percentages can introduce an element of non-linearity, indicated in a hint of an 'S'-tailed distribution – but this problem does not feature in scattergrams of these data, perhaps because the indexes can exceed 100. There seems to be no systematic bias to positive or negative results because of the methods of calculation.

On another point, the data used in this paper on sittings and attendances were tested for normal distributions. Using a test for normality equivalent to the Shapiro-Wilk test, the hypothesis of normality is acceptable for all the Anglican, Wesleyan and Primitive figures, and probably not for the Baptist and Independent data. Statistical transformations of the latter do not much affect the results. Such transformations would also raise interpretative problems. Accordingly, statistical techniques appropriate for non-normal distributions were not used.

5. For example, Coleman, 'Southern England in the Census of Religious Worship', 155.

6. The respective percentages for each North Midland county were Leicestershire: 4.3 per cent, 4.3 per cent; Lincolnshire: 8.1 per cent, 7.2 per cent; Nottinghamshire: 6.6 per cent, 3.5 per cent; and Derbyshire: 6.6 per cent, 4.4 per cent. No single sect was notably more or less likely to return complete sittings figures than the others: the incidence of omissions in sittings figures for the five major denominations (Church of England, Wesleyan Methodists, Primitive Methodists, Baptists and Independents) was in proportion to their respective strength as measured by their shares of the total places of worship. A higher proportion than might have been expected of Anglican Churches failed to provide attendance figures. This is further evidence of the greater difficulties

many of them faced in keeping up attendances compared with the dissenting congregations. The correction method used deals adequately with any relative laxity of Anglican attendance returns, and it is most unlikely that the results are adversely affected. This finding regarding attendances throws more doubt upon the use of 'sittings' data to consider the relative position of the Anglican Church than it does upon the attendance figures, if one assumes that such omission of attendance figures was often due either to the embarrassment of the incumbent, or to an historically decreased population in the relevant parish, or a combination of both causes.

7. This is the problem with J.D. Gay's suggested method for the correction of registration-district level data, although he was himself almost entirely concerned with the county data. See his *The Geography of Religion in England*, pp. 50–1. His suggestion is in principle better, because it involves the use of the sittings data given in the census footnotes for those cases where the attendance data was absent: the sittings data for the absent attendances is calculated as a percentage of the total sittings for that denomination, and the missing attendance data is then calculated accordingly and interpolated as based upon that. (The principle applies also to the calculation of sittings data for interpolation.) This will provide a slightly more accurate interpolation. However, the method breaks down in the cases where neither sittings nor attendance data have been given, or where the total sittings data for the denomination in question are incomplete, even though perhaps more complete than the attendance data. In some unions or counties this difficulty is less apparent than in others. It may be that the ideal correction method would be a fusion of one dependent upon interpolated mean values, and the one suggested by Gay. In any case, because of the relatively small number of omissions in the census, and the fact that different correction methods produce results differing by only a couple of percentage points at the most, it can be shown that the correlations made here are affected to only a minute degree by the different correction methods possible.

8. Ambler, Lincolnshire Returns of the Census of Religious Worship, pp. xxiv, 172. One parson in the later nineteenth century divided his villagers into 'Church', 'Chapel', and 'Church and Chapel'. See D.M. Thompson, 'The churches and society in nineteenth-century rural England: a rural perspective', in G.J. Cuming and D. Baker (eds), *Studies in Church History, 8: Popular Belief and Practice* (Cambridge, 1972), p. 275.

9. Ambler, Lincolnshire Returns, p. xxiv. However, there is evidence to suggest overlapping attendance even for the Primitives. See e.g. the woman whose views were reported in A.R. Griffin, *Mining in the East Midlands, 1550–1947* (1971), p. 45: 'I shall take all my children to the church and have them baptized. They have been baptized by the Ranters but I don't think it's right'. This 'traditional' view of the superiority of Church christenings over those of other denominations was quite common, and applied also to marriages and burials.

10. *Report of the Census of Religious Worship*, 1851, p. clii. Authors have in some cases followed this, or taken two-thirds of the total attendances as roughly equivalent to the total attendants. As far as one is aware, the choice of such a fraction is guesswork.

11. This is also the method used by Coleman, 'Southern England in the Census of Religious Worship'.

12. Of course, this is not to deny that there had over time been much adaptability in the 'sittings' space provided by Anglican churches of early construction, and the relation between sitting and standing space will also have varied considerably over time. See e.g. M.W. Beresford and J.G. Hurst, 'Wharram Percy: a case study in microtopography', in P.H. Sawyer (ed.), *English*

Medieval Settlement (1979), pp. 69–70, on the building sequence of this church from the Anglo-Saxon period to the nineteenth century. Cobbett's complaints about the differences between church capacity and local demand were a constant feature of his *Rural Rides* (1830), and indeed underlay his misfounded belief that the English population had declined markedly in his lifetime.

13. If faults exist in the returns for any particular union, like Leicester, the overall effect on the sort of analysis used here would be negligible. One would of course have to exercise a higher degree of caution if one was describing the patterns within a particular registration district.

14. The two measures used here are also very highly correlated both with the numbers of places of worship given for the Anglican Church in the census, and with the Anglican share in each union of total attendances. The same is true for all other denominations. We can note here that if one conducted this sort of analysis (say, for particular towns) using the 1851 census data as well as data for the same place derived from earlier or later local evidence, comparison of the results would allow many questions to be answered concerning the effects of increased church provision upon church attendances. At only one time, however, the direction of the casual link between the two variables is less clear.

15. An objection sometimes made against the Religious Census has been that bad weather in some regions on the Census Sunday may have impaired the returns. For example, it is thought that rain may have affected rural attendances more than urban, because people in the country probably had further to travel. If this had significantly modified the numbers attending for some denominations in some regions, but not in others, the analysis here would surely have produced lower correlations between the 'attendances' and 'sittings' data, and would probably have done so for all denominations.

Chapter 3. The Geography of Religious Dispersion

1. In 1859 the *Wesleyan Methodist Magazine* spoke of south-east Leicestershire: 'Here are 30 villages, with populations from 100 to 1,000 each – and in another direction there are nearly 20 villages more – in which *there is no Methodism*'. Quoted by D.M. Thompson, 'Church extension in town and countryside in later nineteenth-century Leicestershire', in Baker (ed.), *The Church in Town and Countryside*, p. 437.

2. In passing, one should note that the mid-nineteenth-century strength of the Anglican Church should not be exaggerated. If one takes two-thirds of the Anglican total attendances as an extremely crude indicator of the number of separate attenders, then in the North Midland unions between 7 and 38 per cent of the population were attending Anglican worship on Census Sunday. About 19 per cent of the entire population of the North Midlands would have attended Anglican worship on this day, or, over 80 per cent did not. (By comparison, in Britain in the period 1947–57, one might expect about 5 per cent of the population to have attended weekly the Church of England's services. See G. Sergeant, *A Statistical Source-Book for Sociologists* (1972), p. 120. Or see M. Chisholm, 'Britain as a plural society', in M. Chisholm and D.M. Smith (eds), *Shared Space: Divided Space; Essays on Conflict and Territorial Organization* (1990), pp. 24–5, for 1975 and 1985 adult membership figures, as taken from *Social Trends*, 18 (1988), p. 171.) Using the same two-thirds fraction, about 15–16 per cent would have attended a Methodist place of worship in 1851. About 42 per cent of the population would have attended at some Protestant or other place of worship. (The figure was about 14.9 per cent in

Britain in 1947–57, Sergeant, *Statistical Source Book*, p. 120. If one took Easter Day communicants of the Church of England in Great Britain as a percentage of the 1951 population, the figure would be about 3.7 per cent. See R. Currie and A. Gilbert, 'Religion', in A.H. Halsey (ed.), *Trends in British Society since 1900* (1972), p. 424). The registration-district numbers for the highest-attended Anglican service on Census Sunday 1851 hardly ever rose over a quarter of the population in the North Midlands. Far more often it was about a tenth of the registration-district population, and in Radford fell to as low as one-twentieth. Nevertheless the Anglican Church was almost always stronger than any other single denomination, although this was not so in the Wesleyan strongholds of Hayfield or Horncastle. In many unions the combined Methodist attendances outnumbered Anglican: for example, Louth, Horncastle, Caistor, Glanford Brigg, Gainsborough, Belper, Bakewell, Chapel-en-le-Frith, or Hayfield. The North Midland situation of the Anglican Church in 1851 contrasts noticeably with 'the widespread and deeply rooted survival of Anglican loyalties and practices' in the previous two centuries, as stressed by J.C.D. Clark, *Revolution and Rebellion: State and Society in England in the Seventeenth and Eighteenth Centuries* (Cambridge, 1986, 1987 edn), p. 38.
3. On this see Gilbert, *Religion and Society in Industrial England*, pp. 129–30; Ambler, Lincolnshire Returns of the Census of Religious Worship, pp. xxxiv–xxxvi; G.F.A. Best, *Temporal Pillars: Queen Anne's Bounty, the Ecclesiastical Commissioners, and the Church of England* (Cambridge, 1964); O.J. Brose, *Church and Parliament: The Reshaping of the Church of England, 1828–1860* (Stanford, 1959); P.J. Welch, 'Blomfield and Peel: a study in co-operation between Church and State', *Journal of Ecclesiastical History*, XII (1961), 71–84; M.H. Port, *Six Hundred New Churches: The Church Building Commission, 1818–1856* (1961); K.A. Thompson, *Bureaucracy and Church Reform: The Organizational Response of the Church of England to Social Change, 1800–1965* (Oxford, 1970); R. Currie et al., *Churches and Churchgoers*, p. 60.
4. R. Currie, *Methodism Divided: A Study in the Sociology of Ecumenicalism* (1968), p. 146.
5. On the position of the Anglican Church in the larger towns, see e.g. McLeod, *Class and Religion in the Late Victorian City*; Inglis, 'Patterns of religious worship in 1851', *Journal of Ecclesiastical History*, II (1960), 74–86; Perkin, *The Origins of Modern English Society*, p. 201.
6. Kendall, *Origin and History of the Primitive Methodist Church*, vol. 1, p. 300. As late as 1896, nearly 75 per cent of Primitive Methodist chapels were in the villages rather than the towns. See D.M. Thompson, 'The churches and society in nineteenth-century rural England: a rural perspective', in Cuming and Baker (eds), *Popular Belief and Practice*, p. 273.
7. On rural depopulation, see E.A. Wrigley, 'Men on the land and men in the countryside: employment in agriculture in early-nineteenth-century England', in L. Bonfield, R. Smith, and K. Wrightson (eds), *The World We Have Gained: Histories of Population and Social Structure* (Oxford, 1986); J. Saville, *Rural Depopulation in England and Wales, 1851–1951* (1957); R.F. Peel, 'Local intermarriage and the stability of rural populations in the English Midlands', *Geography*, 27 (1942), 22–30; A. Constant, 'The geographical background of inter-village population movements in Northamptonshire and Huntingdonshire, 1745–1943', *Geography*, XXXIII (1948), 78–88; R. Lawton, 'Population movement in the West Midlands, 1841–61', *Geography*, 43 (1958), 164–7; R. Lawton, 'Rural depopulation', in D.R. Mills (ed.), *English Rural Communities: the Impact of a Specialised Economy* (1973); P.A. Graham, *The Rural Exodus* (1892); A. Redford, *Labour Migration in England, 1800–1850* (Manchester, 1926); W. Ogle, 'The alleged depopulation of the rural districts of England', *Journal of the Royal Statistical Society*, LII (1889); F. Purdy, 'On the decrease of the agricultural population of England

and Wales, 1851–61′, *Journal of the Statistical Society*, XXVII (1964).
8. See the extract from her *My Great Journey to Newcastle and to Cornwall*, printed in Colin Ellis, *History in Leicester* (Leicester, 1948, 1969 edn), pp. 85–7.
9. Wesley′s *Journal*, 31 July 1770 (my emphasis).
10. J. Simmons, *Leicester Past and Present* (1974), p. 126.
11. On the growth of non-Methodist dissenting denominations such as the Particular Baptists, the New Connexion General Baptists or the Congregationalists during the period of Methodist expansion, see Gilbert, *Religion and Society in Industrial England*, pp. 30–42; Currie *et al.*, *Churches and Churchgoers*.
12. However, compare the wider generalizations of W.R. Ward, 'The religion of the people and the problem of control, 1790–1830′, in Cuming and Baker (eds), *Popular Belief and Practice*, p. 253, on the distaste for changes away from an old style of itinerancy within Wesleyanism which 'did play into the hands of the Primitives who harvested a second crop from the Wesleyan mission fields, [and] were always more decentralized and more rural than the Wesleyans'.
13. On the rural evangelizing of the Leicestershire Congregational Association, and the more limited efforts of the Particular Baptists, see D.M. Thompson, 'Church extension in town and countryside in later nineteenth-century Leicestershire', in Baker (ed.), *The Church in Town and Countryside*, pp. 435–6. See also A. Rogers, 'When city speaks for county: the emergence of the town as a focus for religious activity in the nineteenth century', in D. Baker (ed.), *The Church in Town and Countryside*, p. 352.
14. D.M. Thompson, 'The churches and society in nineteenth-century rural England: a rural perspective', in Cuming and Baker (eds), *Popular Belief and Practice*, p. 271, makes the same point, commenting on the success of Wesleyan Methodism in rural areas, despite it being the case that 'John Wesley had no interest in the countryside, either in the farmer whom he regarded as dull and unhappy, or in the farm labourer whom he regarded as grossly stupid.'
15. The numerical strengths of each denomination in the North Midlands can be seen in Appendix B, which gives their total places of worship, sittings and attendances.
16. R.A. Soloway, 'Church and society. Recent trends in nineteenth-century religious history', *Journal of British Studies*, 11 (1972), 153.
17. D.M. Thompson, 'The churches and society in nineteenth-century England: a rural perspective', in Cuming and Baker (eds), *Popular Belief and Practice*, p. 270. As he pointed out, many Methodist circuits encompassed both town and country, and so in religious terms a move to the nearby town would probably not have brought great dislocation for the person involved. See also J. Obelkevich, *Religion and Rural Society: South Lindsey, 1825–1875* (Oxford, 1976), pp. 5–6. In so far as any dislocation did occur, already established connections of faith would probably have helped to ease the person into urban life. Of course, much urban migration was temporary or seasonal, and the extent of short-term 'return' migration from (often industrial) villages to larger Midland towns should be stressed.
18. On the significance of the size of towns as an influence upon the proportion of the population attending places of worship, see H. Perkin, *Origins of Modern English Society* (1978), pp. 200–1. The nine largest towns (over 100,000 population) show significantly lower than average attendance proportions. The 1851 Religious Census material is used, taking the number of attenders as two-thirds of total attendances. He quotes the Bishop of London: 'It is not that the Church of God has lost the great towns; it has never had them (p. 202).
19. P.J. Keating, *The Working Classes in Victorian Fiction* (1979), p. 108. On the

religious situation in the East End, see the account in McLeod, *Class and Religion in the Late Victorian City* (1974), pp. 101–31, 300, 303. Only about 13 per cent of the adult population at the turn of the twentieth century attended any place of worship there.

20. For further discussion of the effects of town life upon religious practice in this period, see in particular McLeod, *Class and Religion in the Late Victorian City*; E.R. Wickham, *Church and People in an Industrial City* (1957); K.S. Inglis, *Churches and the Working Classes in Victorian England* (1963); R. Mudie-Smith (ed.), *The Religious Life of London* (1904); C. Booth, *Life and Labour of the People in London* (1902–3); G. Robson, 'Between town and countryside: contrasting patterns of churchgoing in the early Victorian Black Country', in D. Baker (ed.), *Studies in Church History, 16: The Church in Town and Countryside*, pp. 401–14; S. Meacham, 'The Church in the Victorian city', *Victorian Studies*, 11 (1968); J.H.S. Kent, 'The role of religion in the cultural structure of the late Victorian City', *Transactions of the Royal Historical Society* 23 (1973); R.A. Soloway, *Prelates and People: Ecclesiastical Social Thought in England, 1783–1852* (1969); R.B. Walker, 'Religious changes in Liverpool in the nineteenth century', *Journal of Ecclesiastical History*, 19 (1968), 195–211; N. Yates, 'Urban church attendance and the use of statistical evidence, 1850–1900', in Baker (ed.), *The Church in Town and Countryside*; A. Rogers, 'When city speaks for county: the emergence of the town as a focus for religious activity in the nineteenth century', in D. Baker (ed.), *The Church in Town and Countryside*; E.T. Davies, *Religion in the Industrial Revolution in South Wales* (Cardiff, 1965); D.M. Thompson, 'Church extension in town and countryside in later nineteenth-century Leicestershire', in D. Baker (ed.), *The Church in Town and Countryside*; D.W. Bebbington, 'The city, the countryside and the social gospel in late Victorian nonconformity', in D. Baker (ed.), *The Church in Town and Countryside*; O. Chadwick, *The Victorian Church* (1970, 1980 edn), part II, pp. 218–328.

Chapter 4. Statistical Relationships between Denominations

1. Rutland has been amalgamated with Leicestershire for the purposes of analysis. The figures for its two registration districts are too small to treat it independently.

    The significance levels are also given in these tables. However, such testing of significance is normal only where one is dealing with sample populations, which is not the case here. The significance levels cannot be interpreted in the strict statistical sense, since they refer not to samples but to whole populations. However, they can be taken to indicate the strength of the correlations concerned.

2. The numbers of Primitive chapels and places of worship erected in rural Lincolnshire show sharp rises during the early 1830s, especially after 1834, reaching a peak between 1834 and 1842 (figures calculated from Ambler, *Lincolnshire Returns of the Census of Religious Worship, 1851*). Research on other counties would be necessary to confirm this, but one is tempted to relate this development to the changes in rural social relations brought about by the New Poor Law. On that, see K.D.M. Snell, *Annals of the Labouring Poor: Social Change and Agrarian England, 1660–1900* (Cambridge, 1985), chapter 3.

3. On the Methodist schism of 1849–50, see in particular R. Currie, *Methodism Divided: a Study in the Sociology of Ecumenicalism* (1968), p. 75; or on Lincolnshire, see J. Stovin (ed), *Journals of a Methodist Farmer, 1871–1875*

(Beckenham, Kent, 1982, 1983 edn), pp. 44, 121.
4. Figures calculated from Ambler, Lincolnshire Returns of the Census of Religious Worship.
5. On Nottinghamshire, see G.H. Harewood, *The History of Wesleyan Methodism in Nottingham and its Vicinity* (Nottingham, 1872); J.R. Raynes, *The History of Wesleyan Methodism, Mansfield Circuit, 1807–1907* (Mansfield, 1907); A.R. Griffin, *Mining in the East Midlands, 1550–1947* (1971), pp. 45–6, on the financial and other encouragement of chapels in Nottinghamshire by colliery owners, and their appointment of Methodists as colliery agents; G.M. Morris, Primitive Methodism in Nottinghamshire, 1815–1932 (University of Nottingham unpublished Ph.D. thesis, 1967); B.J. Biggs, Methodism in a Rural Society: North Nottinghamshire, 1740–1851 (University of Nottingham, unpublished Ph.D. thesis, 1975). However, their largely non-quantitative methods do not overlap or enable comparison with those used here.
6. Fitting multiple regression models of the relationships between denominations is also of interest, and will be considered in more detail elsewhere. We might simply note in elaboration of the main argument here that a model using the attendances data, fitted to explain all Methodism combined, using the three predictors of the Church of England, the Baptists and the Independents, produces the following results pointing to the key influence of old dissent:

Predictor	Coef.	Stdev	t-ratio	p
Constant	37.041	4.335	8.54	0.000
Church of England	−0.2159	0.1320	−1.64	0.110
Baptists	−0.5817	0.2576	−2.26	0.029
Independents	−0.7609	0.2910	−2.61	0.013

$R-sq$ = 38.7% $F(3, 40)$ = 8.44.   p = 0.000

7. For further discussion of this technique, see Ya-Iun Chou, *Statistical Analysis: with Business and Economic Applications* (1969), 1970 edn), pp. 649–51, or K.A. Yeomans, *Statistics For the Social Scientist: 2. Applied Statistics* (1968, Harmondsworth, 1979 edn), p. 201–4.
8. On the background of rural anti-clericalism, see in particular E.J. Evans, 'Some reasons for the growth of rural anti-clericalism, c. 1750–c. 1830', *Past and Present*, 66 (1975).
9. On the Anglican opposition to the Primitive Methodists in the Vale of Belvoir, in 'the more purely agricultural parts' of Nottinghamshire, in the Trent valley, Rutland and certain parts of Lincolnshire, generally in places 'much under aristocratic or clerical influence', see Kendall, *Origin and History of the Primitive Methodist Church*, pp. 229, 238, 270–5: 'A good deal of persecution attended the introduction of Primitive Methodism into these parts.' Some of the places most resistant to the Primitives included Kinoulton, Cropwell Bishop, Cotgrave, the area around Belvoir Castle, and especially Bottesford (a parish since demographically reconstituted, showing much demographic stability), which was described by John Harrison as follows:

> This place may be called 'Little Sodom', and I should be surprised if God did not destroy it, was it not for the few righteous souls that are in it. I preached at night, and met with much annoyance from the sinners of this place by their pelting us with dirt and rotten eggs in abundance. (*Ibid.*, p. 239).

(A chapel was finally built here, dated 1820). Persecution also occurred at Shelford (where cottages used for preaching were levelled, their inhabitants evicted: suffering 'persistent, protracted persecution . . . using methods worthy of an Irish eviction agent', but in fact instigated by the Earl of

Chesterfield, *ibid.*, pp. 270–5); Oakham; Bingham; Car Colston Green (where 'gentry were numerous in the neighbourhood, and they watched the progress of the movement with a dislike they took no pains to conceal, *ibid.*, p. 252); Grantham; and Newark. Compared with Nottinghamshire, Rutland and Lincolnshire, there was comparatively little persecution of the Primitives in Leicestershire. Kendall commented on 'this extraordinary difference in the treatment of our pioneer missionaries by neighbouring counties', adding that

> in a very real sense Persecution is 'racy of the soil'; that, in proportion as men are tied to the soil which is not their own freehold, there are the conditions most likely to be found favourable to the propagation of the persecuting spirit. (*Ibid.*, pp. 308–9).

This contention requires further research fully to substantiate it. Some of the most heavily proletarianized arable areas, with large labour-to-farmer ratios, seem to have been very receptive to the Primitives. On opposition to the Primitives, see also D.M. Valenze, *Prophetic Sons and Daughters: Female Preaching and Popular Religion in Industrial England* (Princeton, 1985), pp. 133–6; J. Ritson, *The Romance of Primitive Methodism* (1909), pp. 162, 165–73. On the prior opposition of the Church of England to Wesleyan Methodism in Lincolnshire, see the account of gross violence against an itinerant preacher cited in A. Rattenbury, 'Methodism and the Tatterdemalions', in E. Yeo and S. Yeo (eds), *Popular Culture and Class Conflict, 1590–1914: Explorations in the History of Labour and Leisure* (Brighton, 1981), pp. 34–5. On opposition to Methodism generally, and some of the reasons for it, see J. Walsh, 'Methodism and the mob in the eighteenth century', in G.J. Cuming and D. Baker (eds), *Studies in Church History. 8: Popular Belief and Practice* (Cambridge, 1972), pp. 213–28.

10. On Staffordshire, see J.A. Crompton, *The Pattern of Dissent in Staffordshire in 1851*; and on Warwickshire, see P.S. Ell, *A Quantitative Analysis of Variables Allegedly Influencing the Pattern of Religious Observance in 1851: a Case Study of Warwickshire* (both unpublished M.A. Dissertations, Department of English Local History, University of Leicester, 1988).

11. The mean centre is found by calculating the mean of the x co-ordinates and the mean of the y co-ordinates. These two co-ordinates then mark the location of the mean centre.

Chapter 5. Class, Occupation and Denomination: the Social Structure of Methodism

1. Rev. H.B. Kendall, *The Origin and History of the Primitive Methodist Church*, vol. 1 (n.d. *c.* 1905), pp. 160–2, and p. 117, on the way in which the early 'camp meetingers' did for a time 'cling to the skirts of Methodism'; J. Obelkevich, *Religion and Rural Society: South Lindsey, 1825–1875* (Oxford, 1976), pp. 220–258.

2. For further, but usually very brief and scattered, discussion of the occupational and class differences between denominations, see M.R. Watts, *The Dissenters from the Reformation to the French Revolution* (Oxford, 1978), vol. 1, and vol. 2, forthcoming (containing detailed investigations which will substantially advance understanding of this issue); M. Spufford, 'The social status of some seventeenth-century rural dissenters', in G.J. Cuming and D. Baker (eds), *Studies in Church History. 8: Popular Belief and Practice* (Cambridge, 1972), pp. 203–12; A. Cole, 'The social origins of the early Friends', *Journal of the Friends' Historical Society*, XLVIII (1957), 99–118; R.T. Vann, 'Quakerism and

the social structure in the Interregnum', *Past and Present*, XLIII (1969), 71–91; H. Perkin, *The Origins of Modern English Society, 1780–1880* (1969, 1976 edn), p. 202, on 'the progressive change in denominational allegiance as one moved up – or down – the social hierarchy'; A.D. Gilbert, *Religion and Society in Industrial England: Church, Chapel and Social Change, 1740–1914* (1976), pp. 65–7, 86:

> In every denomination . . . a majority of the adherents . . . came from a common, if variegated, social constituency of skilled and semi-skilled artisans, and in each case the majority was augmented by significant recruitment from shopkeepers and tradesmen, small farmers, and urban and rural labourers.

This sort of statement is symptomatic of current knowledge, for its wording covers virtually all empirical possibilities. See also McLeod, *Religion and the Working Class*, p. 24; D.M. Thompson, 'The churches and society in nineteenth-century rural England: a rural perspective', in Cuming and Baker (eds), *Popular Belief and Practice*; D. Hey, 'The pattern of nonconformity in South Yorkshire', 113, 115; E.J. Hobsbawm, *Primitive Rebels* (Manchester, 1959, 1971 edn), pp. 129–30, 137; Kendall, *The Origin and History of the Primitive Methodist Church*, vol. 1 pp. 97, 162, 298, 300–1; C.M. Elliot, 'The political economy of English dissent, 1780–1840', in R.M. Hartwell (ed.), *The Industrial Revolution* (Oxford, 1970), pp. 144–66; C.M. Elliot, 'The ideology of economic growth: a case study', in E.L. Jones and G.E. Mingay (eds), *Land, Labour and Population in the Industrial Revolution* (1967); J. Kent, *Holding the Fort: Studies in Victorian Revivalism* (1978), pp. 38, 40; R. Currie, A. Gilbert and L. Horsley, *Churches and Churchgoers*. p. 107; Obelkevich, *Religion and Rural Society*, pp. 239–42; E.P. Thompson, *The Making of the English Working Class* (1963, Harmondsworth, 1975 edn), pp. 391, 395; W. Stafford, *Socialism, Radicalism, and Nostalgia: Social Criticism in Britain, 1775–1830* (Cambridge, 1987), pp. 87–8; N. Scotland, *Methodism and the Revolt of the Field* (Gloucester, 1981), esp. chapters 3, 4, and pp. 182–266; Howkins, *Poor Labouring Men*, pp. 40–7; D.R. Mills and B.M. Short, 'Social change and social conflict in nineteenth-century England: the use of the open-closed village model', in M. Reed and R. Wells (eds), *Class, Conflict and Protest in the English Countryside, 1700–1880* (1990), p. 96.

3. The registers used were from the Lincolnshire, Leicestershire and Derbyshire Country Record Offices. In Lincolnshire: Scotter Circuit (1825–1837), Meth. B/Brigg 33.1; Meth. B/Alford/33/1 (up till 25 January 1875; Meth. B/Boston, 33/1 (1844–89); Meth. B/Sleaford/45/1; Meth. B/Grimsby, 33/1 (1843–53); Meth. B/Alford/1/1 (1806–37); Meth B/Louth, 1/1. In Leicestershire: Whitwick and Coleorton, N/M/73/48 (1844–94); Hinckley, Barwell, N/M/142/75; Loughborough, R.G. 4/1444 (1800–13 June 1819); Leicester, George Street, R.G. 4/2325 (MF. 15 (3), (1825–34); Leicester, George Street, R.G. 4/2562; Leicester, Bishop Street, M. 15 (2) (or R.49) (1810–37); Ashby-de-la-Zouch, M.F. 13 (4), (1817–37). In Derbyshire: Bakewell Circuit, J.M. 272 (1807–36); Glossop, R.G. 4/117 (1813–37); Bakewell, D. 1820 J.M. 273 (1807–36); Ilkeston, R.G. 4/33; Duffield, R.G. 4/565.

Where possible, attempts were made to find registers for the two denominations which covered the same districts, to enable comparisons of occupational differences to be influenced as little as possible by variety in the local economies concerned. In practice, this aim is difficult to fulfil, partly because of the general shortage of baptism registers which give occupational details for the very large majority of men being entered in them. Given occupational differences in sectarian sympathies, it is also possible that the registers themselves are predisposed to reflect adaptations of the circuit systems to working locations and parochial employment structures. Such issues call for more detailed research into the occupational bases of denominations, in conjunction with work on the comparative geography and catchment areas of the different circuit systems themselves, research which would do much to advance the local historical geography of religion.

For my simpler purposes here, only six very broad categories have been used to categorize the data. Because of the problems involved, and because of my unambitious use of such data, no systematic attempt was made statistically to control the collection of baptism-register information. Registers which omitted occupations for over about one man in ten were not used, and the large majority of analysed registers, for both denominations, gave this information for virtually all men entered. Because of the Methodist circuit system, these registers provide information from a few hundred villages and towns in the three counties providing data. They also sometimes include places of residence which are clearly not on the circuit involved (even allowing for flexibility and temporary changes in those circuits), which are elsewhere in the county, or even occasionally outside it. Information on occupation for any such entries was also included here.

4. On fertility differences by occupation in the nineteenth century, and the contrasts between mining and textile areas, see M. Haines, *Fertility and Occupation: Population Patterns in Industrialization* (1979). See also the forthcoming work by S. Szreter on occupational variation in the later fertility decline, as based upon the 1911 fertility census. Any possible biases because of high proletarian fertility would be offset also by the relatively high mobility of such occupations, causing them to register baptisms in a wider number of places, thus adding to the likelihood that baptisms of some of their children will be missed using these registers. I am grateful to Tony Wrigley for this point. The method here is the same as that used by him in his research into occupational structure from early nineteenth-century registers.

5. See Currie, *Methodism Divided*, pp. 100–1. His figures were calculated by using deaths as a percentage of the total membership of the previous year.

6. Gay, *Geography of Religion in England*, p. 151. See also pp. 162–3: In Yorkshire and Lincolnshire 'Village Methodism inevitably took on a class-conscious form and the chapel became a symbol of revolt against the squire and the vicar, and a centre where the agricultural labourer could gain his self-respect and his independence'; Thompson, *Making of the English Working Class*, p. 437; R. Moore, 'The political effects of village Methodism', in M. Hill (ed.), *A Sociological Yearbook of Religion in Britain*, 6 (1973).

7. For example, J. Arch, *The Story of his Life, Told by Himself* (1898); G. Edwards, *From Crow-Scaring to Westminster* (1922). On the links of the Primitive Methodists with agricultural unionism, see also Howkins, *Poor Labouring Men*, especially chapter 3; Scotland, *Methodism and the Revolt of the Field*; H. Newby, *The Deferential Worker* (1977, Harmondsworth, 1979 edn), p. 66; H. Gurden, 'Primitive Methodism and agricultural trade unionism in Warwickshire, 1872–5', *Bulletin of the Society for the Study of Labour History*, XXXIII (1976); P. Horn, 'Methodism and agricultural trade unionism in Oxfordshire: the 1870s', *Proceedings of the Wesley Historical Society*, XXXVII (1969).

8. Kendall, *Origin and History of the Primitive Methodist Church*, vol. 1, pp. 298–301.

9. *Ibid.*

10. As based upon Ambler, Lincolnshire Returns of the Census of Religious Worship, 1851.

11. Kendall, *Origin and History of the Primitive Methodist Church*, vol. 1, p. 97. For more detailed discussion of Methodism among the miners of the North Midlands, see A.R. Griffin, *Mining in the East Midlands, 1550–1947* (1971), pp. 45–50, 74; C.P. Griffin, 'Methodism in the Leicestershire and South

Derbyshire coalfield', *Proceedings of the Wesley Historical Society*, 39 (1973), 62–72; J.E. Williams, *The Derbyshire Miners* (1962), pp. 76–9, 107, 118–121: 'Most of the Derbyshire [miners'] leaders of the nineteenth century (and even later) were Primitive Methodists and remained so'. Their trade union meetings were often held in chapels, and biblical texts adorned the banners of the Derbyshire Miners' Association and other mining unions. 'The singing of hymns was so much a part of union business that a special miners' hymnbook was provided for members'; R. Burt, *The British Lead Mining Industry* (Redruth, 1984), pp. 182–3; J.L. and B. Hammond, *The Town Labourer* (1917, New York, 1967 edn), pp. 272, 276: 'the miners were particularly given to Methodism'; although as is clear from J. Ginswick (ed.), *Labour and the Poor in England and Wales, 1849–1851: The Letters to the Morning Chronicle*, vol. 2 (1983), pp. 101–2, the religious inclinations of colliery workers should not be exaggerated. D. Thompson also points to the comparatively low religious attendance figures of the mining districts in Leicestershire. See his 'The churches and society in nineteenth-century England: a rural perspective', in Cuming and Baker (eds), *Popular Belief and Practice*, p. 270. On Methodism predominantly in another coalfield, that of the north-east, see in particular Robert Colls, *The Collier's Rant: Song and Culture in the Industrial Village* (1977), pp. 76–96, 100, 166–8, 196–7.

12. On the conditions and diversity of the framework-knitters, see e.g. *Report from the Commissioners Appointed to Inquire into the Condition of the Frame Work Knitters*, XV (1845); W. Felkin, *An Account of the Machine-wrought Hosiery Trade: its Extent, and the Condition of the Framework-knitters* (1845); and his *A History of the Machine-wrought Hosiery and Lace Manufactures* (1867); G. Henson, *History of the Framework Knitters* (Nottingham, 1831, 1970 edn); T. Cooper, *The Life of Thomas Cooper, by Himself* (1872, Leicester, 1971); W. Jackson, *An Address to the Framework-knitters of the Town and County of Leicester* (Leicester, 1833); A. Temple Patterson, *Radical Leicester: a History of Leicester, 1750–1850* (Leicester, 1954), e.g. pp. 42–9, 115–8, 120–7, 130–2, 291–2, 298–301; F.A. Wells, *The British Hosiery and Knitwear Industry: its History and Organisation* (1935, Newton Abbot, 1972 edn); J. Ginswick (ed.), *Labour and the Poor in England and Wales, 1849–1851: The Letters to the Morning Chronicle from the Correspondents in the Manufacturing and Mining Districts, the Towns of Liverpool and Birmingham, and the Rural Districts, vol II: The Midlands* (1983).

13. See J.A. Banks, 'The social structure of nineteenth-century England as seen through the census', in R. Lawton (ed.), *The Census and Social Structure* (1978); S.R.S. Szreter, 'The genesis of the Registrar-General's social classification of occupations', *British Journal of Sociology*, 35 (1984), 522–46. See also his 'The first scientific social structure of modern Britain, 1875–1883', in L. Bonfield, R. Smith and K. Wrightson (eds), *The World We Have Gained* (Oxford, 1986), pp. 337–54.

14. Howkins, *Poor Labouring Men*, pp. 45–9.

15. The numbers for these separate Methodist denominations are often very small (or commonly there is no recorded presence of them), so making correlation of them independently a doubtful exercise in some cases. The bringing of them together is unfortunate because the result is imprecise. However, in view of the way many historians group *all* Methodist sects together, it can be countenanced here. It has not been possible to locate sufficient baptism registers for these minority Methodist sects in the North Midlands which give near-comprehensive details of occupations, which would have allowed comparison with the Primitives and Wesleyans. The Methodist New Connexion baptism register for Epworth and Crowle (Lincolnshire County Record Office: Meth. B/Epworth and Crowle/84/1, 1853–1903) suggests a surprising predominance of farmers in the sect in that area. The circuit was a largely rural one, mainly between Doncaster and Scunthorpe. Farmers comprised 44

per cent of the males entered, while farm labourers were only 9 per cent. The combined agricultural wage-dependent occupations were only 18 per cent of the total. There were a number of 'gentlemen' and professional men entered. The sect was supposedly radical, self-consciously more intellectual, sometimes termed the 'Tom Paine Methodists', 'tinged with Jacobism', suggested E.P. Thompson, who commented on an earlier period that 'in several places the link between the New Connexion and actual Jacobin organization is more than a matter of inference' (*Making of the English Working Class*, pp. 48–9). It would be of interest to compare these occupational figures with results from other regions, to build up a fuller picture of the sect.

Chapter 6. The Southern Counties – Contrasts and Similarities

1. B.I. Coleman, 'Southern England in the Census of Religious Worship, 1851', *Southern History*, 5 (1983).

Chapter 7. Conclusion

1. E.M. Tranter, 'Many and diverse dissenters' – the 1829 religious returns for Derbyshire', *Local Historian*, 18 (1988), 165.
2. By Paul Ell, Margery Tranter and others in the Department of English Local History, University of Leicester.
3. Everitt, *Pattern of Rural Dissent*; D. Mills, *Lord and Peasant in Nineteenth-century Britain* (1980), pp. 125–8; Obelkevich, *Religion and Rural Society*.
4. M.K. Ashby, *Joseph Ashby of Tysoe, 1859–1919* (Cambridge, 1961), p. 77. N. Yates has commented that 'it cannot be supposed that all those who attended particular churches or chapels lived in the parish or the immediate catchment area' – see his 'Urban church attendance and the use of statistical evidence, 1850–1900', in Baker (ed), *The Church in Town and Countryside*, p. 390. On this see R. Ambler, 'A lost source? The 1829 returns of non-Anglican places of worship', *Local Historian* (1987), 487; his Lincolnshire Returns of the Census of Religious Worship, 1851, pp. lxxiii, 172; and his 'Religious life in Kesteven – a return of the number of places of worship not of the Church of England, 1829', *Lincolnshire History and Archaeology*, 20 (1985), 61, 64:

> Rowston with Sheffield House. . . . It should be observed, however, that there is one Wesleyan Methodist family in the parish, who usually attend their own place of worship in an adjoining village . . . in very many parishes it is the custom for the sectaries, especially among the Calvinists, to go seven or even ten miles distant to worship. The 'Ranters' [Primitive Methodists] also frequently migrate on the Sunday, and form part of the congregations in places where they are otherwise strangers.

With regard to Fulbeck, S. Fane wrote that 'It is impossible for me to state with any accuracy the number of persons connected with this chapel, many attending there from other districts'. See also the returns for Spittlegate, Houghton and Walton. On the distances travelled in Derbyshire, where distances over three miles on very uneven terrain were common, see Tranter, "Many and diverse dissenters" – the 1829 returns for Derbyshire', 163. For another region, see N. Caplan, 'Sussex religious dissent, c. 1830', *Sussex Archaeological Collections*, 120 (1982), 194–5, 199. On the distances walked for religious attendance, see also Kendal, *Origin and History of the Primitive Methodist Church*, pp, 154, 244, 254; J. Buckmaster, *A Village Politician*

(Horsham, 1982), pp. 70–1; Thompson, *Making of the English Working Class*, p. 437. One should also note that persons going to places of worship were exempt from payment of turnpike tolls. Stipulations like this presumed travel for worship. *Steer's Parish Law* (1857 edn), p. 198, citing 3 Geo. IV, c. 126.
5. On the pressures upon labourers to attend the Anglican Church, see e.g. R.L. Gales, *The Vanished Country Folk, and Other Studies in Arcady* (1914), p. 23:

> The labourers and their families all came to church – they would have got the sack if they hadn't. The big farmers had a man at the church door to tell them off one by one as they came in. Any absentee would be reported on Monday morning, and if a satisfactory explanation was not forthcoming he would have to go.

6. For interesting discussion of the problems of such terms, S. Banks, 'Nineteenth-century scandal or twentieth-century model? A new look at "open" and "close" parishes', *Economic History Review*, XLI (1988), 51–73.
7. Flora Thompson, *Lark Rise to Candleford* (1939, Harmondsworth, 1976 edn), pp. 254, 335.
8. The use of very low and zero figures in correlation is not advisable, and would produce problems in the interpretation of results.
9. On the regional complementarity of the Bible Christians and the Primitives, see E.J. Hobsbawm, *Primitive Rebels* (Manchester, 1959, 1963 edn), pp. 136–7; Currie, *Methodism Divided*, p. 102.
10. For example, D. Hempton, *Methodism and Politics in British Society, 1750–1850* (1987). One of the more extreme views on Methodist compromise and pusillanimity was that of Cobbett in *Rural Rides* (1830, Harmondsworth, 1975), indignant at their 'mixture of whining cant and of foppish affectation'. He commented also that they seem to have 'taken the Church *under their protection*. They always pray for the *Ministry*; I mean the ministry at Whitehall. They are most '*loyal*' souls. The THING *protects them*; and they lend their aid *in upholding* the THING' (pp. 187–8, his emphases).
11. Gilbert, *Religion and Society in Industrial England*, p. 120.
12. Some historians, notably E.P. Thompson, have carefully differentiated between different Methodist sects in assessing their political impact, and their effects at different times. But historians have almost never been concerned to identify, distinguish between, and explain the variety of 'Methodist' positions as based upon region.
13. On how old and new dissenting denominations might even reach understandings among themselves on taking districts, see D.M. Thompson, 'Church extension in town and countryside in later nineteenth-century Leicestershire', in Baker (ed.), *The Church in Town and Countryside*, p. 438. See also W.R. Ward, 'The religion of the people and the problem of control, 1790–1830', in Cuming and Baker (eds), *Popular Belief and Practice*, p. 244.

DATE DUE

HIGHSMITH 45-220